SCIENCE FICTION HEROES AND HEROINES

Edited by

David McDonnell

CRESCENT BOOKS
New York • Avenel

RT

This 1995 edition is published by Crescent Books,
distributed by Random House Value Publishing, Inc.
40 Engelhard Avenue, Avenel, New Jersey 07001

Random House
New York • Toronto • London • Sydney • Auckland

Library of Congress Cataloging-in-Publication Data
Starlog's science fiction heroes and heroines / edited by
David McDonnell.
p.   cm.
ISBN 0-517-11950-1
1. Science fiction films. 2. Science fiction television programs.
I. McDonnell, David. II. Starlog.
PN 1995.9.S26S69   1995
791.43′615—dc20   95-17569
CIP

Printed and bound in China

8 7 6 5 4 3 2

30.00

CONTENTS

THE HEROIC WAYS

Just three or four decades ago, of course, it used to be cowboys. But now, and for the last 25 years or so, we all want to grow up to be science-fiction heroes and heroines.

The *Mercury* and *Apollo* astronauts launched it. They climbed into those rickety "tin cans"—state of the art, cutting edge technology for the time—and rocketed off into space, all in an effort to get a mere toenail-hold elsewhere in the cosmos. Visit the Moon. Risk your lives in the quest for knowledge. It's the heroic way.

Watching the astronauts' exploits in the '60s—can it be so long ago?—provided real drama. This was truth, this was happening now, these were heroes for today and the future. Why play cowboys and Indians? Why pretend to be cops and robbers? No, the thing to do, the people to be were the astronauts and blast off into space.

And if *not* Alan Carpenter, John Glenn or Neil Armstrong, why not Kirk, Spock or McCoy? Or just a few years later, Luke, Leia or Han Solo? Picard or Data? Odo, Kira or Janeway?

Vast libraries have already been filled with musings on the significance of those two modern strains of pop culture youth, *Star Trek* and *Star Wars*. Both have ignited the imaginations of millions while—it's the American way—accumulating hundreds of millions in revenue. Both share an optimistic view of events, whether it's a future of sleek starships or the distant past of a time "long, long ago in a galaxy far, far away." No matter what the Empire, the Romulans, Jabba the Hutt or Q may throw at them, despite the evil schemes and the Death Stars and the impossible odds, they *will* prevail. Why? Because they're heroes.

This volume is a celebration of such heroism—fictional heroism, to be sure. It's not quite the real-life heroics of a fireman battling a burning building, a medic giving mouth-to-mouth resuscitation or a teacher patiently helping a child learn to read. Still, these fictional heroes inspire the spirit, their adventures entertain, their actions set an example. They allow us to escape the confines of everyday Earth, to sample what's out there in a far-off tomorrow we will never live to see.

Science-fiction heroes are as old as the genre itself. But the protagonists of those classic novels by SF pioneers Jules Verne and H.G. Wells are mostly faceless heroes. Verne and Wells were more concerned with novels of *ideas* rather than characters—and that's certainly evident when one tries to recall their heroes' names. Wells doesn't bother to give the master of his Time Machine any proper name at all (he's the Traveler). Their damaged men of science, the anti-heroes Captain Nemo and Doctor Moreau, remain mesmerizing, those books' heroes, less so.

That began to change early this century when Edgar Rice Burroughs introduced John Carter of Mars and Tarzan of the Apes, one a proud Virginian swordfighting his way across an alien planet, the other a boy raised by African apes to be king of the jungle as well as a member of Britain's House of Lords. These adventure fantasy heroes—and other earlier creations like H. Rider Haggard's Allan Quatermain and Sir Arthur Conan Doyle's Professor Challenger—pointed the way for the SF characters to come.

And then, thanks to the vanguard genre magazines like *Amazing Stories*, *Weird Tales* and *Astounding*, and later to newspaper comic strips, radio dramas, movie serials, comic books, TV shows, films and even video games, there were a legion of SF/fantasy heroes and heroines vying for our attention. These were people (mostly male) you had probably heard of (even if you had never read or seen their escapades), heroes who themselves remained far more memorable than their own ritualized adventures. You know their names. Buck Rogers. Flash Gordon. Doc Savage. Conan the Barbarian. Superman. James T. Kirk. Luke Skywalker. Mad Max. Jean-Luc Picard. RoboCop. Judge Dredd. And many, many more.

Heroes have always been part of STARLOG, the media magazine founded in 1976 to chronicle the science-fiction universe. Almost 20 years (and 3,000 articles) later, its pages have included many interviews with the men and women (actors, writers, directors and artists) who created these SF/fantasy heroes and heroines for books, movies and TV shows. In this volume, we've collected talks with 24 popular genre figures. These actors did not literally create their heroic alter-egos—writers, of course, originally envisioned the characters—but they have come to *personify* these SF heroes and heroines. After all, how can you mention Spock and not think of Leonard Nimoy?

Since most of those folks have been interviewed by STARLOG's SF-savvy writers more than once over the years, we've combined and updated those chats for a more comprehensive portrait. There have been, for example, at least five separate STARLOG conversations with Arnold Schwarzenegger. The chapter herein unites them all. So, it's a sure bet if more than one writer is credited in the byline, that the chapter involved is made up of more than a single interview.

In the meantime, STARLOG continues to explore the hero and his, or her, world each month. Check out the racks of your local newsstands, bookstores, SF/comics shops or convenience stores for the latest issue.

We invite you to join us there in the pages of STARLOG. It's a great place to read all about, not just cowboys and Indians or cops and robbers, but those characters who we still *really* want to be when we grow up: the heroes and heroines of the science-fiction universe.

—David McDonnell, Editor, STARLOG Magazine

ALIEN NEMESIS

By Adam Pirani and Ian Spelling

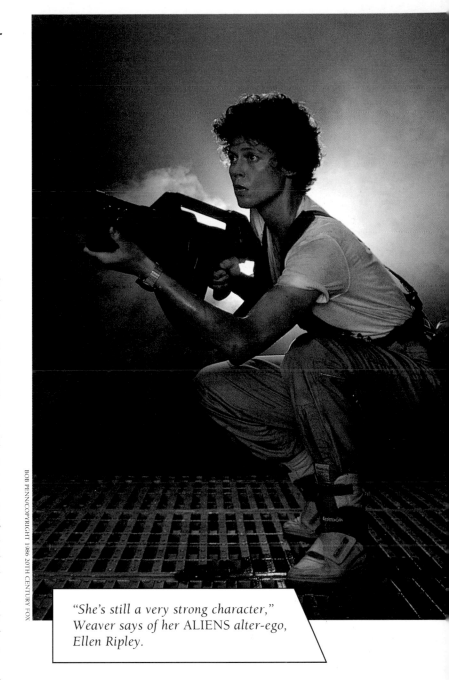

"She's still a very strong character," Weaver says of her ALIENS *alter-ego, Ellen Ripley.*

Begrimed with dirt, her costume torn, Sigourney Weaver sits in the shadow of the massive "drop ship" on Stage D at England's Pinewood Studios. It's clear that for the actress, *ALIENS* is as challenging a movie as *ALIEN* was.

Weaver made her film debut in *ALIEN*, but is now a strong-willed leading actress in her own right. She agreed to reprise her role of Ripley in the first sequel (as well as the later *ALIEN 3*) "because the emotional content of the part is much greater."

"Ripley's situation in the beginning of *ALIENS* just challenged me," Weaver says. "I tried to imagine and comprehend something like that, coming back to a whole different world, and yet, still being haunted by the other one. And Ripley's personal situation is so *bleak*. I know, I'm playing the same character, but I feel she is changed, so utterly, by what happens to her early in *ALIENS*—I don't think she's the earnest young ensign she was when she went into space the first time. So, in a sense, it's a joy to return to Ripley with a whole different set of conditions. In that group of Marines, because she's from another time, she feels like an *alien*.

"She's still a very strong character. They say that originally *ALIEN* was written with a male lead which they changed to a woman—and it's not a bad idea," Weaver laughs, "to try to write women more like men, without sentimentalizing us."

It wasn't just the promise of her role that attracted Weaver to *ALIENS*. "I talked to Gale [Anne Hurd, producer] and Jim [Cameron, writer/director] a lot about *why* they were doing a sequel—I mean, I didn't want to do *ALIENS* just to make 20th Century Fox a lot of money," she laughs. "I wanted to be sure that the people making this movie had the same attitude toward it that I did, and wanted to make a film that would stand on its own and hold up for the people who hadn't seen the first one. There will be people who like the first one better because it's a different director, different vision. But *ALIENS* has its own admirers because it's very well done."

Ever since the release of director Ridley Scott's *ALIEN* in 1979, sequels have been discussed. But the Cameron version was the first approach Weaver considered seriously—although some more humorous continuation ideas had been suggested. "The producers [Gordon Carroll, David Giler and Walter Hill] are friends of mine anyway, and we would get together over dinner and laugh about a sequel," the actress says. "The other idea was that they would open Ripley's little *Narcissus* tomb . . . and she would dissolve into dust. And then they would get someone else to star in the movie.

"But when I read Jim's script, it was almost *all* Ripley, and I was surprised that no one had talked to me about it before. They *could* have *ALIENS* with no Ripley, but Jim wasn't willing to do it without me.

"Jim is incredibly open to things. I always felt that he trusted my instincts and that he had his own very clear idea of Ripley. Whatever decisions I made about her mental and emotional attitude, he has tried to incorporate into scene changes, how we play them, and things like that."

It has been 15 years since Weaver battled desperately against the *ALIEN* in her first movie role. "I was so inexperienced that the first week, Ridley had to tell me not to look into the camera. Ridley and the producers came to New York with a list of actors to see and I was on the list. I really hadn't done any film work, and I remember thinking that I wasn't sure that I wanted to do science fiction.

"Then, they liked me, but I was actually very critical of the script after I read it. When I came back, I was criticizing it and the casting person was saying, 'Stupid woman! Don't you realize this is your big break?'

Each time, it's war—as science-fiction heroine Sigourney Weaver took on the ALIENS in three movies.

"But I think it's better to speak out, to see how receptive people are, and whether they're going to listen to you. With a big role in a movie like *ALIEN*, you have to find people who work together, and I actually found Ridley's vision of Ripley very agreeable. I remember the first costume I tried was too fashiony, so Ridley threw this horrible thing at me that had been found, a real astronaut's practice uniform, and that's the one I ended up wearing. I thought he set up that world so specifically, not as a smooth, shiny 'science-fiction' world, but this dirty, gritty one, and he saw the *Nostromo* crew as sort of outlaws, a group of misfits, and I thought that was a very good concept.

"For my screen test in London, he had a little set built for me, and I did a run-through of the movie. It wasn't really until the day before I tested that I decided, 'Yes, I really want to do this, it's going to be interesting.' I was impressed by the people I was working with. But, when you read the first *ALIEN* script, if you haven't seen the design, for all you know it's a big blob of Jell-O running around—you don't know what it is. When they showed me the designs, I was like, 'Wooow!'—this huge, erotic creature, a wonderful exploitation of everybody's darkest fears. *That* made it for me. I thought, 'It will be beautiful and frightening at the same time.' The majesty, the grace that *ALIEN* has is really unique."

Despite the suddenness of her success in *ALIEN*, Weaver did not come to that movie inexperienced at acting. Born in 1949 in New York City, she attended Stanford University and Yale Drama School. On leaving Yale, she returned to New York and appeared in off-Broadway productions and TV series.

After *ALIEN*, Weaver played a TV journalist in

"ALIEN 3 was sort of a downer," Weaver understates. With an Alien incubating inside her, Ripley leaped to her death.

COPYRIGHT 1991 20TH CENTURY FOX

Although it didn't match the success of the earlier *ALIENS* adventures, Weaver remains "very proud" of *ALIEN 3*.

Eyewitness and an embassy attaché in *The Year of Living Dangerously* opposite co-star Mel Gibson.

"Mel's great, he's just a regular guy," the actress says. "He's very funny, and no one has ever seen him be as funny as he actually is. I would love to work with him again."

With a remarkable range that includes biographical thrillers (*Gorillas in the Mist*) and comedies (*Working Girl, Dave*), Weaver made another mark in the SF/fantasy genre starring as an early customer—and later, a fearsome challenge—for *Ghostbusters* Bill Murray, Dan Aykroyd, Harold Ramis and Ernie Hudson. "My agency in New York suggested me for it, and [director/producer] Ivan Reitman thought, 'Well, I don't know, she's awfully *serious*,' " Weaver recalls. "But I auditioned for him with the possession scene and I really did get possessed. I jumped around the couch, and started to eat the pillows and turn into a dog. I was disappointed when I finally didn't *really* get to turn into a dog in the movie."

Much of Weaver's off-Broadway stage work has been comedy. "My main thing, actually, is comedy—*I* think," she notes. "And of course, Danny, Harold and Bill were so funny because they couldn't understand my motivation—they went, 'You want to do this film with *us*?' From my point-of-view, I was delighted to be in their company.

"There was always so much laughter on the set, and every time I tried to prepare for the icebox scene in *Ghostbusters* where I was supposed to really see something and be afraid, Bill would come over and go [she puts on a weird voice]: 'Ooooooh, *Sigourneee-y*!' He completely wrecked my concentration, but I loved that. I think you do your best work when you're really loose—and you have to be loose with Bill Murray.

"I also saw that it's not just magic and brilliance—those guys really did have to *work*. Not every take is funny, and not every improvised line is the right one. Their humor wasn't just mad blinding talent—although I think they have talent. They really did search to find what would make the scene funny. Working on *Ghostbusters* was glorious."

Weaver enjoyed the whole business so much that she rejoined the entire cast for 1989's *Ghostbusters II*, which remains overall a bit of a disappointment.

Likewise, *ALIEN 3* disappointed some fans. A bleak and depressing film, it took Ripley to a hostile prison planet where she faced the Aliens again and ultimately, with an Alien incubating inside her, chose a suicide leap over Alien motherhood.

"It was sort of a downer," admits Weaver. "Let's face it, it was a '90s picture, very character-driven and bleak. I really like the fact that all three of them have a different spirit, and I think Ripley was feeling a little tired, which is one of the reasons I thought this picture should end it for her.

"I'm very proud of the film. In fact, we did awfully well. It made more than $200 million internationally, so Fox, no doubt, is starting to think about an *ALIEN 4*, obviously without me. I think the reason that it didn't do well [in America] is that after the success of *ALIENS* and *Terminator 2*, people wanted *ALIEN 3* to be another Jim Cameron film.

"We didn't want to do the same thing again. I really like the fact that each one was different. When I actually talked to Jim about *ALIEN 3*, he said he loved the film, and he was so gracious. He said, 'I would have done exactly the same thing [as director David Fincher did]. I would have thrown away everything I worked so hard to establish and done my own story.' So, I think, in time, Fincher's *ALIEN* film will be appreciated more, but I'm very proud of it now."

As a veteran of a quartet of genre films, a science-fiction heroine, does Weaver enjoy SF and fantasy movies? "I've never been asked that before," she responds. "I love fantasy. And to a certain extent, most films are fantasies.

"It's much better for an audience to want us to destroy or vanquish the Alien—it's a very traditional thing, like killing a dragon. It's much healthier, to me, than movies about going to Vietnam and killing a lot of people—it's disturbing, somehow, the way people react to *those* fantasies.

"There is a feeling that these films are all special FX, and yet Steven Spielberg said to me once, 'I really like *ALIEN* because I know all about special FX—I know how everything is done—but when I watched that film, I *forgot*, because the actors in it made it so real for me that I stopped thinking about the FX.' And," says Sigourney Weaver, "if Steven Spielberg stops doing that, then we've accomplished something."

THE ROAD WARRIOR

By Randy & Jean-Marc Lofficier

In *Mad Max Beyond Thunderdome*, Max is older and he's more world-weary," says Mel Gibson. "I think he's also much more open, open to change. He's a better human being. That's a process that happens during the film. It's his journey of character."

It is refreshingly cool inside the tunnel passageway between the Bartertown set and the rest of the Homebush State Brickworks in Sydney, Australia where scenes of *Mad Max Beyond Thunderdome* are being shot. Due to the almost unbearable heat outside, everyone who doesn't *have* to be on the set is in the tunnel, trying to get comfortable.

Extras, resembling refugees from some war zone, wander here and there. At one point, a particularly scruffy fellow, with very long, dirty, greying hair walks in and sits down, wiping the sweat from his face. He is wearing only a pair of torn leather pants. Resting there, amongst the colorful crowd, there is nothing especially striking about him. Few fans would readily identify this bare-chested man as the star of the *Mad Max* trilogy and the *Lethal Weapon* movies, Mel Gibson.

Mad Max II, known in America as *The Road Warrior*, was a worldwide hit, and contributed to making Gibson a superstar. In *Beyond Thunderdome*, he reprises the part, with this third film jointly directed by George Miller and George Ogilvie. "I don't worry about stereotyping," says Gibson. "I always fill in the time with other roles."

Indeed, Gibson's other roles have included not only *Lethal Weapon*, but *The Bounty*, *The Year of Living Dangerously*, *The Man Without a Face*, *Forever Young*, *Braveheart* and *Maverick*. Gibson shows no sign of impatient self-importance or "stardom." He waits for the shot to be set up, just as uncomfortable as everyone else. He jokes and talks with the crew, exchanging banter about the harshness of the previous five grueling shooting weeks in the Coober Pedy desert. He may be the star, but he acts just like one of the guys.

When it is finally time to shoot his scene—Max's arrival in Bartertown—Gibson gets up and walks to the set. It is fascinating to see him transform himself from an amiable set companion to the cold and deadly desert wanderer known as Mad Max. Gone is all the earlier good-naturedness, replaced only by steely self-control and a sense of menace.

Gibson describes how he prepares himself for his role as Max. "It's your basic kind of preparation," he says, "you read, you discuss and you draw on ideas in a pool. Many other actors just sit down and chat it over. Sometimes, it really doesn't come to a finished thought until right before you do it. Other times, not even then, or it happens by mistake. But if you understand the basics, or the foundations of this particular world that your character is in when you set up how one in this environment would behave and react, then, of course, you're halfway there."

COPYRIGHT 1980 AIP

The face of Mad Max: *Gibson first caught SF fans' attention in this Australian import. His voice was dubbed for American release.*

Did he hypothesize on what happened in Max's life between the events of *The Road Warrior* and *Beyond Thunderdome*? "Yes," Gibson answers, "but not in great detail. The world finally ran out of juice. The cars wouldn't run anymore. So, Max went out and caught some camels, and survived any way he could. He shot little animals. He came across people, and they traded a few things. There's not much civilization out there. His is basically a nomadic existence."

In Max's tough post-apocalyptic world, one must change to survive. Max's gentle side, highlighted in the first film (in which Gibson's voice was dubbed for its American release), is now gone, rubbed out by years of endless fighting. Or is it? Gibson wonders whether Max has done things that he might once have been ashamed of, or if simply, Max can't feel shame anymore. "It's purely a matter of survival now," the actor observes. "One thing about the character, even though he's a killer, is that he *does* have a code of ethics. But you see, that code of ethics—how will I put it?—is adjusted for this environment where killing can be justified.

"His family has become something from another era, another world, something that he now finds abhorrent. Yet he just cannot do something like killing Master Blaster [the villain]. It's something that would bother his conscience, then he would feel ashamed. Or maybe not. Max *would* kill Blaster, except that something makes him stop. He himself doesn't

What's love got to do with it? The legendary Tina Turner (as Auntie Entity) menaced Gibson Beyond Thunderdome.

There's both message and action to the third movie. "That made it more interesting for me to do," Gibson admits.

And in Mad Max III: Beyond Thunderdome, *he's even more heroic. Is there a* Mad Max IV *in his future?*

even know what that something is. He hates it in himself. It's his weakness, or he thinks it's his weakness. But in fact, it's probably the only thing that singles Max out from the rest of the scum."

Finis may not yet have been written to this science-fiction hero's saga, but Gibson carefully considers just what might prompt another follow-up. "I wouldn't do a *Mad Max* film no matter what," he announces. "It would definitely have to be something that was going somewhere else. For instance, *Mad Max II* was removed from *Mad Max I*. It was better, it was neater, it was a different kind of story. And *Mad Max III* has evolved into something much bigger. It's a much broader tale and deeper as well.

"So, it's not like doing the same story again. In fact, *Mad Max Beyond Thunderdome* is a very different kind of film. Although Max is the obvious link, which makes the films into a series, they're all so different that he could almost be a different character. What each of the films is trying to say, I think, is different. Yet, I feel you could almost show them in one block and they would still work as one whole, big story."

Mad Max Beyond Thunderdome operates on several levels. It is a non-stop adventure, but also a modern myth fashioned by co-writers George Miller and Terry Hayes. "What they're trying to say is very clear," Gibson explains. "They're marrying the two things very smartly: the message and the action which goes along with it. It's not shoving it down your throat. The fact that this film has a message also made it more interesting for me to do. It means you must work harder for the point. The other two films tended to be slightly nihilistic!"

Gibson is full of praise for director Miller, who shared the job with Ogilvie because he sees himself more as an action director than an actor's director. But Gibson disagrees. "George Miller is very good," he says. "He doesn't think he is, but he is. The dominant force in him is as an artist and a filmmaker, not as an actor's director. He achieves perfor-

mances through framing. He can do that so well he can alter you somehow and it works even better."

Mad Max Beyond Thunderdome is Gibson's third collaboration with Miller, but the actor is certainly *not* bored. "George is always coming out with little surprises and new things," he comments. "And that's good because I know it's exciting to work with George. He's not selfish with his knowledge at all. It rubs off on you. There's a simplicity about him. I find the same thing in most people who are fairly brilliant at what they do. They have the knack of being able to undo the complexitites, just focus on the basics, and build up from there."

The actor is equally complimentary about co-director Ogilvie. "George Ogilvie has the characteristic of really being able to talk to actors. He's learning a lot of film techniques from George Miller, so that they complement each other rather well. There's no ego involved here, you see, only healthy stuff, which leaves great freedom in the exchange of ideas. Two heads are better than one, if the two heads can handle it."

When choosing a project like *Maverick* or *Forever Young*, Gibson studies it closely. "I've always considered pretty carefully what I've done," he maintains, "except for a couple of occasions. And that was in the beginning. But that's where you learn. You have to burn your fingers a couple of times. Now, I always look at it from the most basic way I can possibly think of it—emotionally and just how it hits me. I have to like a script better than many other things in order to do it. I don't have a preconception of what I would or wouldn't like to do."

With *The Man Without a Face*, Gibson made his directorial debut. "The key to directing is to really learn how to edit," he says. "Provided that you have all those other things, you know, about motivation and camera technique. There's a lot involved and you have to get that all together. At first, I didn't know whether I would be any damned good at it."

Of course, he didn't know if he would be "any damned good" at acting either when he began. "Of course not," Mel Gibson says. "But that just happened. I didn't push it. I'm not into planning anything."

REBEL PRINCESS

By Robert Greenberger

Sometimes, you just can't escape *Star Wars*. Just ask Carrie Fisher, who portrays Princess Leia in that galaxy far, far away.

"With *Star Wars* on cable TV about every 20 minutes, I see myself regularly and it's almost like it's *not* me anymore," she says quietly. "I'm not as recognizable as Mark Hamill or Harrison Ford, so I only get a sense of *Star Wars'* importance when a child recognizes me and becomes speechless. Kids don't think I'm on this planet. Very little children even believe Princess Leia is a *real* human being—that I live in outer space.

"It's just so big," she says of the international *Star Wars* phenomenon. "I feel like if I hauled out my American Express card, it would have to say Princess Leia because this reaction is so universal." Her involvement has dwindled, though; *Return of the Jedi* marks her last appearance in the *Star Wars* saga.

"I've almost literally grown up around George Lucas," she explains. "I was terrified and petrified the first time I met him." Actually, Fisher had been working before *Star Wars*. The daughter of performers Debbie Reynolds and Eddie Fisher, she began singing at her friends' Bar Mitzvahs at age 12. By age 15, she was performing in the chorus of the Broadway revival of *Irene*, which starred her mother.

Fisher's film debut came in 1975 in *Shampoo*, the Warren Beatty comedy in which she played a sexually aggressive young girl. A movie career beckoned, but Fisher chose instead to spend two years in England at the Central School of Speech and Drama.

Explaining how she was cast in the role of science-fiction heroine Leia Organa, Fisher indulges in a whimsical flight of fancy. "I always like to think I was sitting in Schwabs [legendary Hollywood drugstore], with that particular hairstyle, and George came in and said, 'Gee, *that's* just what I need.'" In reality, she was home for vacation, attending a giant "cattle call" for actresses jointly held by director Brian DePalma and Lucas. DePalma was casting *Carrie*, while Lucas searched for Princess Leia, the only major female character in his film.

"The dialogue for our screen test was even more complicated than that in *Star Wars*," Fisher recalls. "The sentences were *sooo* long. You didn't know what you were talking about, so finally you would ask, 'George, in my motivation for this scene, you must tell me, *what* is a Bantha? What am I actually saying?' You just have to give it up and trust that you mean what you're saying. So, I went and read after all that

"*I was desperate to do* Star Wars," Fisher recalls of her screen test, "*because it was the best script I had seen.*"

Events became darker in the trilogy's middle film, The Empire Strikes Back.

English training and was able to get the dialogue out of my mouth.

"Lucas *never* spoke during the interview. Brian DePalma talked and they would see people for maybe two minutes. George sat behind his beard and laughed. I, in no way, behaved like a 19-year-old. I was *not* intimidated by either of them. I was fearless. I didn't feel any desperation about my career, but I *did* want that job."

Several weeks later, Fisher did get invited back to read again for both directors. She did a videotape test with Harrison Ford, who had already been signed to play Han Solo. In the end, DePalma hired Nancy Allen (whom he later married and divorced), Amy Irving and P. J. Soles, while Lucas selected Fisher.

"When I saw the script, I never figured they would hire me, because I'm this short, sort of plump little thing. The script said Leia was this beautiful princess—she's just beautiful. I was desperate to do *Star Wars* because it was the best script I had seen, it was a fairy tale."

Making *Star Wars* and its two sequels was hard work for everyone involved, especially the actors who had to pretend that they were firing actual ray guns and watching real planets blow up. "I've done so many scenes to a piece of tape because they add whatever the monster is later," she explains. "We shoot our guns, but we never see what falls over. I watched my planet blow up as a blackboard with a circle drawn on it held by a bored Englishman.

"I'm always slightly surprised about what I was reacting to earlier. There's nothing like that in real life."

During the first film's production, one thing which continually concerned the cast was the dialogue, much of it written in a Shakespearean manner. "It's what Harrison used to say: 'You can type it, but you can't say it.' We used to go to George and go, 'Say this.'

"When I first met Governor Tarkin [Peter Cushing], I wanted to say my line glibly, but George gave me my direction. I read the dialogue, my God— how would *you* say, 'I recognized your *foul stench* when I came aboard'? Since I had just been to school in England, the first film is funny to me in that I sometimes sound English, but that's the only way you can say it with absolute authority. This is *real* talk. It was the only time George gave me lengthy direction other than 'Faster, more intense.' "

Fisher laughs about Princess Leia, a character who's an aggressive female, almost one on the guys. "I have other generals, I shoot guns and behave like a soldier. It's almost a male sort of thing. Well, I am the *only* girl in an all-male-made movie," Fisher announces. "Sometimes, I would say to them, 'How about a big cooking scene, baking some space food, or how about me sewing my costume back together? A shopping scene, maybe on a mall planet? Give me a girl friend and we'll talk about how cute Han is.' There are no moments where Leia is stereotypically female.

"It is interesting that they give the female so much power," says Fisher, and drops her voice, which takes an ominous tone as she adds: "And in *Jedi*, I got even more!

"But I always felt Leia had a strength that was more based on anger than a strength that was power. Her strength came from bitterness about wanting to eliminate evil from the universe. It was interesting because I wasn't sure how to approach her in *Jedi*. Initially, I thought it was unusual because I was much more feminine this time. I've watched the first

RALPH NELSON JR./COPYRIGHT 1983 LUCASFILM LTD.

Return of the Jedi *provided not only classic derring-do but a skimpy outfit for Fisher. "It was George Lucas' idea," she confides.*

film on TV and at times, I feel like I am under orders and I keep saying the lines like, 'You came in that thing?' And I was insulting people.

"I asked George in *Jedi* for some sort of a drinking problem . . . not really a drinking problem, but I said, 'Look, Leia lost her parents and planet in the first film and in the second movie, a very close friend becomes frozen. By the third movie, I must be totally exhausted. I've been chased for who-knows-how-many-years.' I figure I'm ready to go, 'Hey guys, I *can't* do this anymore. I'm going to get my hair done. You handle it.' "

Princess Leia does, however, lose some of her regal bearing as a slave girl in *Jedi*, serving the loathsome Jabba the Hutt. "He forces me to put on new clothes," Fisher explains, "some handy slave girl outfit that he had in all sizes. We were shooting the interiors in England during the coldest winter they've had. I

17

"Very little children even believe Princess Leia is a real *human being, that I live in outer space*," Fisher explains.

stunned, grimacing, though it looked to them that I was smiling. I swear, I'm not smiling. This is *not* fun! I had to kick people and hit them. It isn't natural for me to have fist fights with people."

Unlike *The Empire Strikes Back*, most of the major characters were involved in scenes answering questions or resolving situations from the previous two films. Fisher got into the act and received secret scenes on special color-coded pages in sealed envelopes. She laughs, "The days when we would shoot the secret scene, they would ask the crew *not to listen*. It's fun, like the Academy Awards. We've learned to get the secrets and learn them fast. You must. It was harder on *Jedi* because some of these secrets were acting secrets, instead of 'NO, STOP. LOOK AT THAT!!' But you wouldn't get the script pages for those scenes until the last minute, and whereas I might want to work on them, I couldn't. There's no time."

Fisher says she is always looking for roles which provide her with the opportunity to do different things and has sampled stage—including a stint in *Agnes of God*—TV and movies like *The Blues Brothers* and *Hannah and Her Sisters*.

"There have never been any roles that I've seen and said, 'I *must* play that role.' Certain things are so difficult to do, *Agnes of God* included. I have proved to myself that I *could* do it. In new projects, I just look for something that I've never done before. I also look for something that I could learn from the role," she says.

Mostly turning away from acting in recent years, Fisher has carved a second career as a novelist (*Postcards from the Edge*, *Surrender the Pink*) and screenwriter (she "punched up" *Hook*'s Tinkerbelle scenes).

was walking around in sandals and the fewest clothes I've ever worn in the movies. I was shocked when I found out it was all *George's* idea."

Over the course of the three *Star Wars* films, it has been Fisher who primarily directed the growth of Princess Leia Organa, although Lucas created the initial background. Fisher takes great pains to make her character consistent. She says she is "unfortunately" a perfectionist, always working toward a better next performance.

She was aided on all three films by strong directors: George Lucas, Irvin Kershner and the late Richard Marquand. "Out of the three, Richard was the only one who was an actor, so he had a different perspective than Kersh," Fisher observes. "Kersh is also very much an actor's director. It's interesting working with all of them because they've all been so different. *Jedi* was a lot like shooting *Star Wars* because of the speed—we shot it very quickly. We would shoot rehearsals, particularly the action scenes so we could see where the squibs [explosions] are. When they do go off, that's not acting, we really *do* react because we're stunned. That's why the Endor battle scene was so hard, because I was always

Fisher usually receives copies of the *Star Wars* merchandise and continues to marvel at the proliferation of toys and other stuff. "I don't know what to do with it all," she admits. "What am I supposed to do with 25,000 Boba Fett dolls? I give them away at Halloween.

"It made me laugh so much the way they portrayed me in the foreign movie posters. There's someone with giant hooters and a lot of leg and it doesn't look like me at all. The Italian poster had this blonde, buxom, leggy person. Me, I'm 5'1" and my legs end almost right after they start.

"People think I'm taller. I meet people and they say, 'You're sooo short,' as if I didn't know this fact. They say, 'You look taller in films,' or 'You look much prettier in person'; they expect me to have a gun somewhere. Maybe I should insist in my contracts that I always wear a gun or carry an explosive."

Nevertheless, Carrie Fisher feels that there is more to learn and more to show through her acting. "I'm still working on myself as a human being," she says, "which to me is important. That's something that I can separate. It's healthier that way."

SCIENCE-FICTION HERO

By Brian Lowry, Thomas McKelvey Cleaver, Kim Howard Johnson, Will Murray and Marc Shapiro

If there's one person who personifies the contemporary science-fiction hero, it has to be Arnold Schwarzenegger.

SF fans know him best as *Conan the Barbarian*, the *Terminator*, the *Predator*'s human prey, *The Running Man*, that guy with *Total Recall*. And when it comes to all these roles, Schwarzenegger does indeed have total recall. Take Conan, for example.

He believes the Robert E. Howard-created hero is one who, no matter what the ratings considerations, must remain a savage. "Can you slaughter people and never see blood? Is it possible? You must have battles. That's part of life, war and *Conan*."

It quickly becomes apparent that Schwarzenegger is remarkably frank, good-natured and affable. And after looking at him, it's not all that hard to understand. He can afford to be. Although now out of body-building and into acting, Schwarzenegger, at 6′2″, is still a formidable sight. When he walks into a room, he looks like a tank camouflaged in a business suit. And business is certainly what his screen career has been all about.

"Since I didn't have financial troubles [after his bodybuilding career], I didn't have to go out and act to make a living. I could wait for projects which would help me one way or another with my career," he explains. "Even when I did *The Vil-*

The second Conan film, Conan the Destroyer, *is "action-action-action." It may not be Schwarzenegger's last time as the barbarian hero.*

Schwarzenegger was literally unstoppable as the killing machine from the future known as the Terminator.

And, indeed, although the actor's sword has remained in mothballs, Universal Pictures continues to push the barbarian with a Conan attraction on the Universal Studios Tour. There's also a finished script ready for whenever Schwarzenegger feels it'll be time to be Conan again.

It's an experience one wonders why he would want to repeat. His memories of *Conan the Barbarian* are laced with pain. Due to his massive physique, finding a stunt double to match him was all but impossible. Instead, the actor did almost all of his own stunts in that first Conan film—leaping off a 50-foot tower, getting mauled by wolves and wrestling a 36-foot, hydraulically-operated snake.

Additionally, Schwarzenegger was bitten on the head by the camel he punched out, fell down and cut his forehead badly in the cave where he discovered the Atlantean sword, and was nearly decapitated while lensing the orgy chamber battle. When the axe wielded by former Oakland Raider Ben Davidson was parried by Schwarzenegger's sword, the axe blade flew off, striking Schwarzenegger's shoulder and missing his head by inches.

Still, when it comes to finding the bright side to such a situation, Schwarzenegger seems more like Little Orphan Annie than barbaric Conan. "The only way you could do the role is by going through the physical pain in reality, to really get its feeling," he explains, noting the difference between acting and reality. "Then, you don't have to fake the facial expressions. I mean, if you get attacked by wolves, you *look* scared—you don't have to make funny faces anymore.

"I was never too concerned about the dangers. [Director] John Milius would always tell me, 'Whatever accident you have, remember the pain is temporary, the movie is permanent.'"

He survived—and the movie became a success. According to Schwarzenegger, based on the feedback he has received: "Not *one* guy who is a Conan fanatic or a Robert E. Howard freak, didn't like the movie. That's the biggest compliment you can get—to please the people who know the stories and love the character. [Executive producer] Dino de Laurentiis *didn't* want me to be in the movie," Schwarzenegger contends. "He didn't like me playing the part. He didn't like the way I talk. And then, Milius said, 'Well, listen, if we don't have Arnold play Conan, we have to *build* one; so, if you have time to build another Arnold, then go ahead.'

"The second Conan movie is really very different from the

lain—I read the script and knew it was not interesting—I thought I would love working with Ann-Margret and Kirk Douglas; I could *learn* from them. I wanted to work with Hal Needham, because he's a very different kind of director and I would learn.

"This is the way I choose my roles: I had to find something in the package that interested me or which could move me up."

After receiving positive reviews for *Stay Hungry* and *Pumping Iron*, his waiting strategy paid off with 1981's *Conan the Barbarian*—a serious part suited to his physique—which reached blockbuster status thanks to its box-office performance worldwide. A sequel, *Conan the Destroyer*, followed. Schwarzenegger played basically the same heroic character (although he bore a different name for legal reasons) in *Red Sonja*.

"He is a fun character to play, to bring to people. I could see myself playing him until *Conan X*. I could do a *Conan* every few years and other projects in between them. It all depends. If *Conan V* makes $100 million, they'll probably be stupid enough to do a sixth one."

first one," Schwarzenegger attests. "*Conan the Destroyer* is just action-action-action from the first scene! When we were making it, I asked the director, Richard Fleischer, 'How can you get all of this into one movie?'" Adding credence to his concern, he notes that Fleischer's first cut was more than three hours in length. The film was trimmed to focus almost entirely on action.

Looking at the second film, Schwarzenegger recognizes that Fleischer had a somewhat easier task than Milius. "John had to take time to tell the audience about the character of Conan, who he was and why he was this way. So, due to that, there were times when the movie moved slowly," the actor explains. "Richard had all of that given to him. He didn't have to establish that history. He could concentrate on the action and adventure."

Following his time as the villainous, albeit starmaking, *Ter-*minator, Schwarzenegger returned to heroism with such films as *Commando, Raw Deal, Red Heat, Predator* and *The Running Man.*

"After I had finished reading *The Running Man*, I said to myself, 'That would be an interesting part to play.' It stuck in my mind," Schwarzenegger recalls.

But another actor (Christopher Reeve) already had the part in the movie version of the Stephen King ("Richard Bachman") novel. Then, Reeve dropped out and Schwarzenegger found himself literally in the running—playing the science-fiction hero who's a contestant in the ultimate game show of the future. The only goal is to survive, an awesome challenge when the host employs a formidable team of enforcers, the stalkers, whose job it is to hunt down and kill contestants on *live* television.

"The actual battle scenes between the Running Man and

In Total Recall, *Arnold Schwarzenegger was again a science-fiction hero—and a man without a memory who used to be a bad guy.*

the Stalkers are very unique," explains Schwarzenegger. "I'm fighting these guys with my bare hands, while they use all kinds of vicious equipment, like flamethrowers. There's one guy with a chainsaw; Dynamo shoots electric current at people to kill them. He also has this very ugly vehicle, with spikes sticking out in front, that's meant to run people down and kill them. Those are the things that I—and the rest of the Running Men with me—have to fight against.

"I enjoyed doing *The Running Man*, and it was a very sophisticated kind of film, with many other things besides just action. I liked the whole idea of the modern gladiator, the government being in control of the Network and fixing the contest, and the show being organized to prevent people from rioting and protesting by keeping them glued to the TV set. I was very impressed with the idea of having Richard Dawson as the show's host, the evil guy—Richard really played that *so* well."

As for *Predator*, "I was pleased we had John McTiernan to direct—he was perfect for the job," Schwarzenegger says, noting that some studio execs didn't much like the movie during its production and were shocked by its box-office performance. "SF movies, futuristic movies and action movies are really the way to go. Thinking back, *Predator* came out really wonderful. It was a really good horror and action movie. I didn't really care about genres that much," he says, "but somehow I end up many times in SF films. I love science fiction, the whole idea of futuristic SF, magic and all those kinds of things in films."

Specific parts don't matter to Schwarzenegger. "Playing a villain or a good guy always depends on the script—I'm wide open for any of those things. I'll play whatever seems to be an interesting character.

"Someday, I would like to do a hardcore Western, and a good, traditional war movie—any of those things would be appealing. Comedy, in general, appeals to me more than anything else," notes the actor who has earned laughs with Danny DeVito in *Twins* and *Junior* (as a pregnant man) and made such comedic action films as *Kindergarten Cop*, *Last Action Hero* and *True Lies*. "When a film has comic relief, people mention those moments more so than the shootouts or action scenes."

"Compared to the T-1000," the actor notes, "I am definitely the good guy" in Terminator 2: Judgment Day.

Strangely enough, in his SF action blockbuster *Total Recall*, Schwarzenegger wasn't quite sure who he was playing. "I really don't know," he admits, taking a Brobdignagian cigar out of his mouth long enough to flash his engaging gap-toothed smile. In fact, Schwarzenegger plays two roles—Doug Quaid, the seemingly ordinary construction worker in 2075 America, who dreams of living on the red planet Mars, and Hauser, a mysterious alter-ego who may be the real person with Quaid an imperfect identity, just a dream.

Quaid's life is shattered when he goes on vacation via Rekall, Inc., a service that implants computer-generated memories of any action you can't afford to take in reality. But Quaid's vacation goes horribly wrong: The memory implants don't take and everywhere he turns, people try to kill him.

"The interesting thing about this is that I play a character who's always changing from this normally behaving man into this frightening machine with tremendous will," Schwarzenegger explains. "He didn't know he had it in him."

Schwarzenegger has not one, but two love interests: Sharon (*Basic Instinct*) Stone as Quaid's "faithful" wife, Lori, and Rachel (*Fort Apache: The Bronx*) Ticotin as Melina, a resistance fighter on Mars.

"It is great because it fits in this movie. I don't want an actress in my picture if she's just selling tickets. I want her only if she has a position that's believable and she belongs in the movie. Rachel has been the biggest surprise to me. She has been absolutely terrific as an actress, and also as an athlete because she comes from a dancing background. She has gone way beyond what any women has done that I've seen in movies."

Total Recall, based on the Philip K. Dick short story "We Can Remember It for You Wholesale," is a futuristic thriller that superimposes a Dickian milieu on an Alfred Hitchcock ian dramatic structure. It's a mindbending surreal exercise in paranoia, with Schwarzenegger particularly relishing the metamorphic quality of his dual role.

"Starting with an average guy who does his work eight hours a day and transforming into a guy who's really pulled by ambition," he explains, "and little does he realize that he's drawn to something much bigger than he expected. We're talking about saving a planet. So, it becomes a race and Quaid goes insane getting there. The earlier character—Hauser—is obviously the interesting one. This was the most complex character I've ever played—a character of purpose and complex emotions."

Such a dualilty is something that would enliven Schwarzenegger's next SF film. He had already played *the* relentless, evil *Terminator*, now why not a *good* version?

The inevitable movie, 1991's *Terminator 2: Judgment Day*, reteamed Schwarzenegger and his *Terminator* director, James Cameron.

"Jim and I *always* knew that we would do it," the actor announces. "During the first few weeks [of shooting *T2*], we did a lot of the dialogue scenes. How much dialogue and human communication did my character have in the first movie? So, it was obvious from the first day on the set that *Terminator 2* was going to be a more difficult film for me.

"Also, it was difficult in that my character, as the film progresses, shows subtle signs of humanity, and we were not shooting the scenes in any kind of order. Jim and I would discuss where the changes in the character would be, and I would constantly ask him, 'Is he too human now or is he not human enough?'"

One aspect of his character that Schwarzenegger is not totally committed to is the good-guy nature of this *Terminator*.

"He's good only in the way he ends up," the actor responds. "Anyone who does the damage the Terminator does in this movie could *hardly* be considered kind and gentle. He's more dangerous than good.

"What makes this Terminator different from my character in the first film is that, this time, he's trying to fit in with his environment. As he goes along, he's adopting human behavior patterns. This makes for a change that has him going from being a straight machine to something that's attempting to be human but not quite getting there. Only to a certain extent does he get humanized, but there are those scenes, like when he makes the comment that he wishes he could cry, that we get tiny glimpses of his humanity. He's still very dangerous and threatening, but this behavior does begin to change as this film goes along, and compared to the T-1000 [Robert Patrick], I *am* definitely the good guy in this movie."

For Schwarzenegger, reuniting with director Cameron and co-star Linda Hamilton has been "like turning back the clock to a very happy time. Working with Jim now has been totally different from when we first worked together. He has been more fanatical about details than he was years ago. He's more adept at fine-tuning the acting, and he catches things now that he might have let go them. He's more of an actor's director than he ever was before, and he has concentrated on making every scene something special.

"I had so few scenes with Linda in the first *Terminator*, and those were only when I was chasing her or shooting at her. The nature of this storyline has brought us together, and she has been a pleasure to work with."

As for the original *Terminator* and its sequel, Schwarzenegger looks back on them as phenomena that struck an intellectual nerve with both critics and audiences.

"The *Terminator* movies are a perfect example of the right creative elements and perfect timing coming together," he says. "The story, the look, the director, the actors—they were the elements that went into making what could have been a normal action movie into something magical."

Everyone connected with *Terminator 2* insists that this will be the last *Terminator*. But Hollywood being what it is, it comes as no surprise when Schwarzenegger says, "Never say never. Jim and I are both too busy to even think about a third *Terminator* film.

"It could very easily be that people would want a third one. *Terminator 2* does *not* indicate to me that there's an end to the story possibilities. According to what we know about the future, there were *hundreds* of Terminators built. This story could go on forever."

As for Schwarzenegger's own future, there are numerous possibilities: *The Crusades* (a period action film), *Sweet Tooth* (a comedy/fantasy in which Schwarzenegger would inherit the family job, being the Tooth Fairy), a *Planet of the Apes* revival, *Sgt. Rock* (a WWII movie based on the comics hero) and a *Total Recall* sequel.

No matter what roles he accepts, he insists he's looking for one thing.

"Challenge. And to make sure the movie's entertaining for people. Then, it doesn't matter *what* it is."

Arnold Schwarzenegger agrees that while he always likes to stretch himself as an actor, he knows exactly what his audience expects. "I have to give the audiences what they enjoy seeing," he says, "while I try to bring in a little something new, with different movies, different time periods and all those things. But what's important is to entertain the people—everything else means nothing."

STARSHIP CAPTAIN

By David McDonnell, Lynne Stephens,
Bill Florence and Marc Shapiro

This man has presence. You can feel it as soon as the door opens. He dominates the room as he does a stage, though he seems far smaller than the commanding figure he portrays on *Star Trek: The Next Generation*. In person, he's warm and very, very low key. Not at all the intimidating Captain Jean-Luc Picard, Patrick Stewart is a friendly guy.

"I've done very few films," he notes, "yet, three of the films I've done are science fiction. One was *Lifeforce*, one was *Excalibur*, one was *Dune*. So, I have a great deal of science fiction in my background. Also, I've done many classics, particularly Shakespeare, and there's a lot in his work which deals with experiences philosophical and scientific.

"People ask, 'All those years as a classical actor, 25 years with the Royal Shakespeare Company, don't you feel that doing *Star Trek* is a comedown?' I can safely say with absolute certainty that all of that was *preparation* for *Star Trek: The Next Generation*. I could *not* do this job if I had not done that other

stuff. So much of what I've done before has been preparation for Jean-Luc Picard."

His preparation, of course, to play this science-fiction hero has included pivotal roles in those three single-word titled fantasy epics. In 1984's *Dune*, Stewart played Gurney Halleck, warmaster to the Duke Leto Atreides (Jurgen Prochnow) and one of the teachers of his son Paul (Kyle MacLachlan).

In Frank Herbert's *Dune*, one of the recognized masterworks of SF literature, Gurney Halleck is an important character. But in the David Lynch film version, Halleck's role is somewhat diminished. "Oh yes," Stewart agrees, "the role was never as important or as significant in the film as in the book. Halleck is a musician, poet *and* warrior. Well, all you really saw of him was the warrior side.

"David Lynch *did* shoot the book, but it just didn't get on the screen. It's a good film, but I suspect there's an even better film in all that David shot. I don't think David Lynch's work was seen at its best in *Dune*."

The actor also took up the blade in a world of swashbuckling fantasy, albeit in the grim, muddy and bloody Camelot of 1981's *Excalibur*. "It has some of the finest images I've seen on the screen," notes Stewart, who played Leon de Grance, "especially those early sequences before the Golden Age arrives when it shifts from black to silver armor.

"At that time, I found the director, John Boorman, a little remote, very, very preoccupied with images and the look of the film. But those were the early days of filming for me and I was probably a little timid. I enjoyed my character and the writing very much. And I was working with people I had known for a long time like Helen Mirren, who I had known in England for 20 years."

His other venture in science fiction came as Dr. Armstrong in 1984's *Lifeforce*, directed by Tobe Hooper. "I have to say, of the movies we've been discussing," Stewart remarks, "Tobe Hooper was the director to whom I got closest. I liked him very much and I admired his work. As compared to my experiences with David Lynch and John Boorman, Tobe was much more accessible. And even though my part was not large, he spent a lot of time with me. He was a very good listener and he would incorporate the actor's ideas."

One of Stewart's most satisfying experiences began while shooting the 1985 film *Lady Jane*. Looking for something to occupy his time off the set, he came across Charles Dickens' 1843 novel *A Christmas Carol* and began to read. "And I was suddenly aware that, although I *knew* the Christmas Carol—everybody knows the story of *Christmas Carol*—I had never actually *read* it," the actor admits. "I have a feeling that probably applies to the majority of people. So, I read it, and before I had finished, I knew that all of my impressions about *A Christmas Carol* had been substantially adjusted.

"I had thought of it as being a rather sentimental and somewhat melodramatic, whimsical, Victorian Christmas story. What I saw in the book was a very powerful piece about the power of redemption, as well as being a very tough uncompromising picture of the harsh social conditions in Victorian London.

Says Patrick Stewart of Captain Jean-Luc Picard, "The best heroes are the ones with flaws."

"Most particularly, I was moved by the almost-Shakespearean major theme, which is that of a man leading a bad life who's given a vision of his future and invited to change. Not *changed*, but to change himself and acquire redemption."

A short time later, Stewart read portions of the novel at a fundraiser and then fashioned a one-man show from the book, an acclaimed production in which Stewart has now played Los Angeles, London and Broadway. And the actor plays *everyone*—including a dead-as-a-doornail Jacob Marley, Bob Cratchit, those dancing Fezziwigs and Ebenezer Scrooge himself.

A Christmas Carol "is difficult for an audience. They have to sit for two hours and watch *one* actor, without costume, with no set or props and minimal furniture, not just *telling* a story, but inviting them to use their imaginations in quite a demanding way," Stewart explains. "The show won't work unless an audience is prepared to come a long way to meet me in the performance."

Stewart has found miserly Ebenezer Scrooge the most challenging to portray "because he's the character who undergoes the most change. And in the same way that a major dramatic character in a fine play will have an arc of development and change, that applies to Scrooge. If Scrooge doesn't work, the show doesn't work.

"The other character that gives me a lot of difficulty is the Ghost of Christmas Yet To Come. He barely exists. He's a pointing hand and little else." Stewart must shoulder alone what he considers to be a trio of responsibilities each time he takes the stage in *A Christmas Carol*.

The first, he says simply, is "telling the story. The next thing is to keep them interested, not to bore them. It's the worst thing an actor can do. And, after that, it's necesary that the audiences are *changed*. I see it as my responsibility to send an audience out of a theater with a different perception of the world than the one they had when they came in."

In his adaptation of Dickens' fantastic tale of redemption, Stewart communicates three primary themes ensconced in large doses of creativity and humor: "You cannot do good in the world until you first do good to yourself. You have to correct the imbalances in yourself before you can begin to look outwards. *A Christmas Carol* also tells us not to despair. That's a powerful message."

A Christmas Carol, *Dune*, *Lifeforce* and *Excalibur* are all fine, but it is, after all, *Star Trek: The Next Generation* that interests most fans. Stewart first caught the eye of that show's

Despite its physical discomforts, "I enjoyed being the Borg," Stewart confesses. He wanted life as Locutus to last longer.

producers at a lecture at UCLA, meeting with Gene Roddenberry in October 1986 as the series was slowly shaped.

"I didn't meet anyone from *Star Trek* again until April 1987. I assumed I would be part of a new crew. It was only a few weeks before my final reading," Stewart says, "that I knew I was being considered for the role of the Captain. He's a man of authority, of responsibility. I was fascinated with the idea of playing a man of such power.

"Actually, I knew what *Star Trek* was. I had watched it with my children. But I didn't know what role *Star Trek* played, particularly in this country, in every area of social, cultural and political life. This was first made clear to me in the week that I accepted the part. A friend of mine in Los Angeles asked, 'Patrick, how does it feel, to be going to play an American icon?' "

Almost as soon as he was signed, the comparisons to William Shatner and James T. Kirk began, "I *never* had a problem with Captain Kirk," Stewart avers. "Many other people tried to *impose* a problem on me. I was uneasy about that.

"Until our show aired, every meeting, every interview, every contact on the street was always, 'How is your show going to be different? How are you going to compare? Are you the new Captain Kirk?' Those were impossible questions to answer. I knew what we were doing had a totally different personality. With *Star Trek: The Next Generation*, we are not replacing anyone; we are simply what we are. What had been before is still there. Nothing has been taken away; it will always be there.

"For 25 years, I played roles in Shakespeare that actors have been playing for 400 years before me and that will be played by actors long after I'm dead. So, what is there to get upset about?"

Stewart's classical training—he remains an associate artist of the Royal Shakespeare Company—didn't, he says, go to waste in his weekly TV role. "*Star Trek* is epic in nature," he explains, "as has been a lot of classical work that I've done. *Star Trek* is drawn on a very big canvas. We are truly a heroic series, and I mean that quite seriously in the Pyrrhic sense of heroic. The style of our language is not absolutely naturalistic language: it's somewhat heightened. Gene Roddenberry's work has always had that quality about it. The Bridge of the *Enterprise* is very much like a classical stage: it is dramatically organized, and I often feel it when I walk the Bridge. And," he says, sensing a comic connnection, "being accustomed to years and years of wearing tights without pockets in them, the

In Star Trek Generations, two Captains—and two legends—meet. Stewart and William Shatner had a grand time working together.

Starfleet uniform has come as second nature. You have no-where to put your hands."

As for actually taking the part that has brought Stewart science-fiction fame, it was a number of details, rather than any single impulse, that led to Captain Jean-Luc Picard. "As we often say with a stage play, it is very often the role that is the attraction," he explains. "The part represents a major change in the style of my career, and I've always been an actor who has found contrast, especially *violent* contrast in my work, to be irresistible. It appeals to me to do something which is unusual, unexpected or outside my range. So, the prospect of doing an American television series was intriguing, particularly *one*—and this is very significant—that seemed to me was dedicated to dealing with *ideas* as well as the usual formula of relation-ships, plot, regular characters.

"Therefore, the leader in the 24th century was especially interesting. And undeniably, having been a classical stage actor for most of my life, which means that one may get lots of ar-tistic and spiritual fulfillment but very little in terms of earning a living, the appeal of a TV series which I never had any doubt would be successful, was obviously very attractive." There is one more reason why Stewart accepted the role, he reveals, chuckling. "I don't think my children would ever have forgiven me if I turned it down."

Of course, Stewart did take the role, kept it and made it his own. Now, more than seven years and 178 episodes later, there are countless intriguing *Trek*s to remember.

In "The Best of Both Worlds," a two-parter widely con-sidered by many fans as one of the very best of *The Next Generation*, Stewart relished portraying the newly-transformed Borg Locutus but disliked the role's physical demands. Playing a Borg "was very uncomfortable. It was a four-hour makeup job. And of course, once it was all on, movement was very difficult—*sitting* down or *lying* down or *standing up*.

"But I enjoyed being the Borg. I had hopes that Picard would go *on* being the Borg a bit longer. I thought it would be a lot of fun for Picard to be marauding around the galaxy for several episodes, destroying everything and beating up the uni-verse."

The actor enjoyed working on "The Drumhead" with vet-eran classical actress Jean (*Spartacus*) Simmons. "She's one of my heroines. Her performance was marvelous, and she was such a warm, hard-working and dedicated person on the set. Of course, we've had many marvelous guest performers, but it was especially exciting for me to have Jean, and to be going on a kind of 'head-on' with her."

In such episodes, viewers have had an opportunity to wit-ness the evolution of the *Enterprise*'s Gallic commander. Over the years, "he has deepened, become richer. There are more facets to his character," says Stewart. "Picard has opened up a good deal. We've found that he has a sense of humor, that he has all kinds of passions and enthusiasms for curious, un-expected things. We've seen him in a couple of romantic relationships. We've seen his guard down, and we've seen him vulnerable. It was always my intention *not* to set out to create a perfect hero. I think the best heroes are the ones with flaws. So, I've had a lot of fun finding the flaws for Jean-Luc."

Another phenomenally popular *Next Generation* episode was "The Inner Light" in which Picard lived a whole other life in some 22 minutes as Kamin, iron weaver of the planet Kataan. In a case of art imitating life, Stewart's real life son Daniel played Batai, Picard's son on Kataan.

"The work Daniel did in that was his *own* work," says Stew-art with fatherly pride. However, both Stewarts "ran the lines together and talked about the scenes, because the Captain Picard I was being was not the Captain Picard that would be on the ship, but a man who has lived 40 years in another environ-ment. That's what Daniel and I talked about: 'What kind of father would Picard be if his life had changed so radically, and therefore what kind of son he would have.'"

The experience of working with his only son "was *very*

satisfying and exciting for me," Stewart emphasizes. "If you're going to have a child who becomes a performer like you, to be sharing a professional situation together is *deeply* rewarding."

Not surprisingly, Stewart claims the Hugo award-winning "Inner Light" as his favorite fifth season episode, although his reasons continue beyond his son's appearance. "It was a fascinating script, and it gave me the opportunity to explore a different kind of Picard. What would happen if someone's environment was changed dramatically? How would that person develop? That was extraordinarily interesting."

Other episodes captivate Stewart. He's fond of "Darmok," likes "10010011" and remains intrigued by "The Perfect Mate." In that story of Picard delivering an alien woman to an arranged marriage, Stewart found it moving "to see Picard, against his judgment and wishes, finding himself becoming attracted to a woman he could never have, with whom he could never be. The pressure that put him under made for a very interesting episode."

He's also very proud of "The Offspring," co-star Jonathan Frakes' directorial debut. This tale of Data's efforts to build a daughter, Lal is well-loved by fans. "As a piece," Stewart says, "it represents the very best of what *Star Trek: The Next Generation* is."

But, "All Good Things . . ." come to an end—and so did the series, culminating in the finale of the same name. It was an exhausting experience for Stewart. "In those final two hours," he says, "I was in every single scene and shifting between time periods. It was a difficult time for me and, towards the end, I got so tired that things became a little bit raw and rough for me. But that last episode turned out to be a very satisfying one."

Equally satisfying is the new career opportunity that *The Next Generation* offered Stewart. He made his directorial debut on "In Theory" (in which Data falls in love) and helmed four other episodes ("Hero Worship," "A Fistful of Datas," "Phantasms" and "Preemptive Strike").

"My favorite directing episode, like one's first love, would have to be the first, 'In Theory.' I was a virgin on that episode and those seven days [shooting it] were the most exciting of my career," Stewart says. "I was lucky to have Brent [Spiner] as my leading man and a fabulous guest star performance from Michelle Scarabelli. And finally, I was lucky that 'In Theory' had no big set scenes, no Klingon halls and no shoot-outs. I was left simply to concentrate on structure and camera movements and more than anything else, to work with the actors.

"Beyond 'In Theory,' nothing could match the thrill of directing a Western ["A Fistful of Datas"] with Worf, Alexander and Troi facing a Western town filled with Datas on the Holodeck. Directing that episode provided me with an enormous opportunity to have a lot of fun. Working from sun-up to sundown on the Warner Bros. lot, on its Western set with three cameras rolling was the most exciting day of my life."

Finally, of course, this *Enterprise* crew made the leap to the silver screen with *Star Trek Generations*, a movie adventure that includes them all (and Guinan) as well as a troika from the classic *Trek* (Kirk, Scotty, Chekov) and a villain played by Stewart's old RSC colleague Malcolm McDowell.

"I always felt that the biggest challenge in making the first *Next Generation* movie was to make the best film that we could first and to make the best *Star Trek* movie second," Stewart says. "I didn't want something so elitist that it could appeal *only* to fans or to those people who have been watching the series. I wanted it to be a movie that someone who had never heard of *Star Trek* could sit down and enjoy and not feel excluded. In advance, I felt that would be the biggest challenge."

Some fans expected fireworks from the teaming of Stewart with William Shatner. Stewart *didn't* share those expectations. "I felt that having the two Captains share screen space was something audiences would enjoy seeing," he says. "I didn't know Bill very well, and there had been all those stories about his attitude toward *The Next Generation*, that he was opposed to it. But, I was lucky enough to spend some time with Bill on a plane ride back from an industry convention. In that hour, we got to know one another. We talked about our lives, personal things and what *Star Trek* had meant to our careers. I was delighted to find out what a sensitive, intelligent and gentle man Bill was. When the time came for us to work together, I felt it would be a good experience and it was."

Patrick Stewart himself clearly *does* quite often see the world from an amused point-of-view. His is the demeanor of an actor reveling in his chosen profession, and although his creative muses or demons have urged him, over the years, to spiraling levels of activity, they don't seem to have curdled his obvious pleasure in performing. "All I know is that I *have* to act. It's a compulsion. I'm driven to it. I wouldn't say that I would *die* if it were taken away from me, but a large part of me would shrivel up."

Why is acting such fun? "Ask me that again in 20 years' time. I'm gradually nudging towards an answer to that, but it'll take a good many years before I have it worked out. *Maybe*, when I do, I shall want to stop acting."

Picard lived a whole other life in less than a half-hour in the Hugo-winning episode "The Inner Light," a Stewart favorite.

HEROIC ANDROID

By Joe Nazzaro and Marc Shapiro

"Data has become more and more human as time has gone on," Brent Spiner declares, "but he is still a machine after all." The *Star Trek: The Next Generation* actor is referring to the various changes his character has undergone over the series' history.

"I'll tell you," the actor says, "it was an established journey that his character was going to be on from the very beginning. The point of departure was the word 'Pinocchio,' which was in the pilot, and was Gene Roddenberry's concept. After discussions with him, I agreed completely that the character would evolve through the years towards the humanity he seeks. Through being among humans for seven years, he has been able to synthesize their behavior, and as Gene said, at the end of the journey, Data will hopefully be as close to human as

possible, and still *not* be human. That's the way it has gone.

"Data, of course, *has* become more human," he says. "That has been the thrust from the very beginning. Once the similarity of Data to Pinocchio was planted in everybody's minds, the people on the show knew we would try to create an arc that would have Data come as close to being human as possible without ever accomplishing that goal. That has been the journey Data has been on."

And it is a journey, complete with often contradictory emotions, that at first, had more than one *Star Trek* fan comparing one SF hero to yet another, in this case, Data to Mr. Spock. Spiner disagrees with the Spock comparison.

"I don't think I'm *The Next Generation*'s equivalent of Spock. In fact, I'm exactly the opposite. I'm a heightened character like Spock. I supply information like Spock does. But, there's a big difference.

"Spock is half-human and does *not* want to be human, while Data is not any part human and desires nothing more than to be human. So, in that sense, I think Data is the antithesis of Spock."

Whatever Data is, Spiner agrees with the notion that few episodes went without Data being at the hub of what's happening in the *Star Trek* Universe.

"I don't necessarily think I'm the hub of the show," Spiner points out. "But, Data is like the Shakespearean chorus; the one who's around to comment on the action, the humanity and what's going on in general in each episode.

"Data is an enigma. He's obviously a machine. He has considerable strength and an unbelievable memory. He's a totally logical machine but, over the course of the show, there has always been that question mark. How really human is he, and how human will this series allow him to become?"

Although Spiner has worked on *The Next Generation* for its entire seven year-run, his interest in the show, now itself metamorphosizing into motion pictures as *Star Trek Generations*, hasn't diminished with time. "We're still grappling with interesting ideas and concepts. They have to filter through characters we already know fairly well, but it's not like doing a Broadway show, where you do the same show every night. Doing different scenes every day, and different dialogue, particularly with this role, where you never know from week to week what you're going to be doing, makes it more interesting."

It's the writing that Spiner credits in large part with the success of *The Next Generation*. "I definitely have a dialogue with the writers," he maintains, "and I don't think there's any dramatic work that's done that *doesn't* depend on the writing. It's the old cliché, 'If it ain't on the page, it ain't on stage,' and that's really true. No matter how good an actor you think you are, you cannot make bad writing fly. It just won't happen.

"I've taken jobs in my life where I didn't think the writing was particularly good, but I felt confident enough that I could make it interesting, and I was absolutely wrong. If the writing is not there, then nothing's there.

"In terms of how I play it, I already have a nice base with the writing, but I also have a certain amount of freedom in the way I interpret it. They don't sit on us in the way we interpret it at all. I don't think I've ever gotten a note about how I played a scene, that I played it wrong, or should have played it another

Becoming more human throughout the TV series, Data (Brent Spiner) finally got emotional in Star Trek: Generations.

way. It never happens, so obviously they have the same degree of respect for what we do as we do for them."

Faced with the impressive body of work he has helped create, Spiner is hard-pressed to choose which of his *Next Generation* episodes might be considered true classics. Could the actor, for example, select a videocassette of his best work to show a friend or family member who hasn't seen the series? "Gee, I don't know, I don't think I would show them just one, because I've had so many episodes, and I'm not sure which I like the best. Really, for the most part, it's when I've been given the opportunity to do more than just Data.

"I don't think it was one of our best episodes, but 'Brothers' offered me the best opportunity I've ever had. I was able to play three different characters at once [Data, Lore and Dr. Soong]. There were many problems that had to be solved in order to play a 100-year-old man, but it was very exciting.

" 'Measure of a Man' was a great episode, and I also like 'The Offspring,' which was Jonathan's [Frakes] first directorial piece, and a really nice episode. I had a great time doing 'A Fistful of Datas' for Patrick [Stewart, who directed it], because I got to play five different characters, and there have been episodes that I haven't been heavy in that I liked quite a bit.

Two generations of Star Trek *heroes teamed in* Next Generation's *"Unification" as Spock (Leonard Nimoy) met Data.*

The game's afoot in "Elementary, Dear Data" with an android Sherlock Holmes and his Watson, Geordi La Forge (LeVar Burton).

'First Contact' was a really nice episode, as was the two-parter 'The Best of Both Worlds.' "

Unlike many of his peers who've taken exception to the Emmy Awards' snubbing of *The Next Generation* actors, Spiner is more pragmatic. "You have to dismiss it," he says. "First of all, it isn't so important, although it might possibly be beneficial on a career level. I suppose it's nice to be recognized; I'm not saying I wouldn't like it. It would be swell if someone gave me an Emmy nomination, but I think it's a difficult show to award in that area. One, it's science fiction, and there's usually a taboo on that to begin with. Two, it's written in a style that's so unusual and incomparable to anything else.

"As far as I'm concerned, at the root of it is the fact that I play a comic character in a dramatic series, and there really isn't a category for that, so I don't think that much about it. When

Emmy time rolls around, I always check out who has been nominated, and say, 'Gee, I thought I gave a better performance than that,' but then you say it really doesn't matter, because the truth is, awards are *not* about recognizing fine work. Awards are about advertising, which is about money.

"If I ever gave the performance of a lifetime, and it *wasn't* recognized by my peers, I might be hurt, but I've *never* given the performance of a lifetime, so I don't think too much about it."

While Spiner has resigned himself to being recognized and even approached by the occasional fan, he still hasn't come to grips with being a household name. "Sometimes it's comfortable, and sometimes it's not. If I'm in public, and I'm sitting in a restaurant, and someone comes over and says that they like the show, that's very pleasing.

"There is a dark side to it too, that nobody told us about, and I'm not sure it really existed when I was studying to be an actor. The obsession is the downside to it, but that only has to do with my private existence and my home. If there's anything I don't like about fame, it's that I *do* get phone calls and letters at my house, and that makes me uncomfortable. As far as being in public, though, and being recognized, it's part of the game and a very pleasing part."

Another price of fame is the occasional tabloid or magazine article that presents the celebrity in an unfavorable, or in some cases, completely inaccurate light. While Spiner has yet to be abducted by aliens (in real life anyway), or meet Elvis Presley in the parking lot of his local McDonald's, he was subject of a

magazine article which portrayed him as a lonely workaholic who hadn't had a date in some time. "That was a shame," says Spiner, recalling the story. "You know, after I read it, I felt so sorry for myself. I mean, I knew I was pathetic, but I didn't know I was *that* pathetic!"

Getting serious again, Spiner admits things aren't so bad. "Oh no, I have a very nice life. Certainly compared with 99 percent of the history of the world, I have an exceptional life. And I don't take Data home with me—as soon as I wash the makeup off, I'm me again."

As to life after *Star Trek*, Spiner says, "There are other things I would like to do, like not wearing gold makeup. I've been acting professionally since 1969, I've played many parts, and this happens to be about the best, not just because it has massive exposure, but because I've also played about 15 other characters on the show. It hasn't been as limiting as I thought it might be, taking a series job, which I really didn't want to do for a long time, but I couldn't ask for a better part.

"In terms of typecasting, I'm not really worried about that, because there aren't that many good android parts out there, but I do wonder about what's to come.

"I don't have any fantasy role I would like to play," Brent Spiner announces. "I think I've already played the fantasy part, because for me, playing a character who plays other characters is about as fantastic a role as I could hope for.

"I would like to keep doing stage work and whatever film or television I can do until I'm somewhere in my 100s."

SECOND-IN-COMMAND

By Marc Shapiro

She has never watched much television and never been much of a fan of SF, fantasy and horror films, but if you laid Claudia Christian's genre film and TV credits end to end, they would stretch down a very long city block. And, at the block's end, you would find Christian scratching her head and wondering "Why?"

"I don't know why I keep getting cast in these things," acknowledges the actress in even, slightly melodic tones. "Over the years, I've gotten typed as a person who can play both the strong woman and the crazy woman, and I guess that's what the people who make genre films and TV are looking for."

Christian's talents were definitely what the producers of *Babylon 5* sought, and the result is that the actress is projecting her quiet, tough-as-nails image as the space station's second-in-command, Lt. Commander Susan Ivanova. At the end of what Christian describes as a "pretty efficient 12–14 hour working day," the actress is a bit candid about what's happening on the set.

"I'll bet you if you look closely at the show's first few episodes, you'll notice how I have a tendency to stand real stiff and pull at my uniform jacket. Because I don't watch much TV, I didn't know I was doing a perfect imitation of the way Patrick Stewart acts on *Star Trek: The Next Generation*, until some friends brought it to my attention."

Originally, Christian had no intention of making *Babylon 5* her base of operations. But, following lukewarm reception to the syndicated SF series' two-hour pilot and the decision to recast certain roles, the show's casting director called Christian and asked if she was interested in becoming a Lt. Commander.

"They sent me a few scripts and I thought, 'Wow! What a great role!' So, I went in to audition and got the part."

But the 28-year-old actress claims that, even with the role all but hers for the taking, there was some apprehension. "Frankly, I had done a lot of television in the past and was now actively pursuing film roles. Doing television, in a sense, seemed like a step backwards. Plus, I didn't want to get into an ensemble situation with 12 people and end up getting only three lines a week," Christian says. "What ultimately sold me was the fact that my character was *not* a secondary role and that there *was* room to grow. The bottom line was that I figured that if the show was successful, what did I have to lose? If it wasn't, at least I would have spent my time constructively."

Lt. Commander Ivanova is a multi-faceted character—fighter pilot, Russian Jew. It's a role that's at once familiar and, as Christian explains, working on different character levels.

"Susan is definitely militaristic in her education and dedication. She's serious and professional but not necessarily cold. But there's also a great deal of turmoil with this character that'll become evident as the episodes unfold. She's the youngest person on the station and she has been given a command post that someone her age doesn't normally get, so she's constantly faced with having to prove herself. She comes across as very confident and professional on the surface but, underneath, we're finding out that she has been

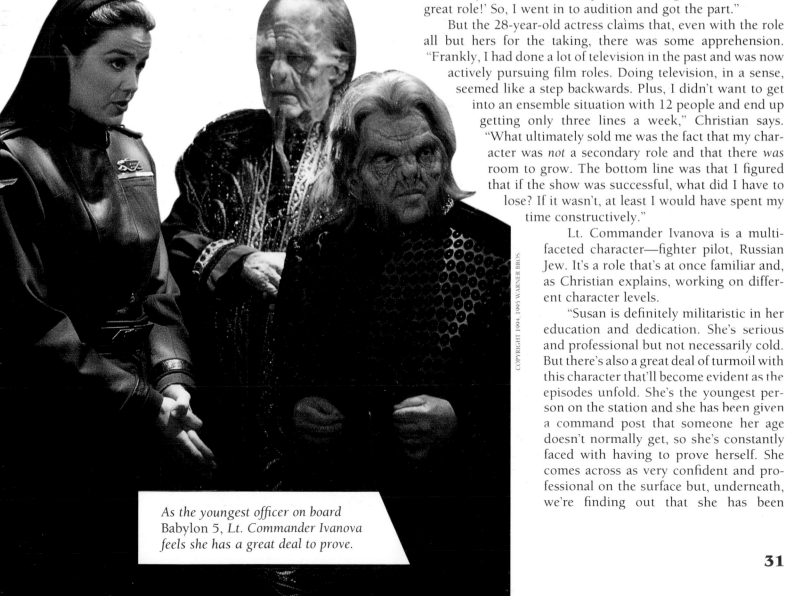

As the youngest officer on board Babylon 5, *Lt. Commander Ivanova feels she has a great deal to prove.*

through a lot. If she were to break down, it would be a *very* big breakdown."

Ivanova's character template is consistent with those of other science-fiction heroines. But Christian feels that Susan is more than merely a clone of ex-*Enterprise* security officer Tasha Yar or *ALIENS'* tough-gal Colonial Marine, Vasquez.

"She is very different from the typical science fiction women. Ivanova is very sardonic, very wry. She's very well read, she's poetic. She loves jazz. As time goes on and she gets more comfortable with her surroundings, you'll see a really interesting, colorful woman. In fact, there's so much going on with Susan that the only role she *is* playing is when she's in command."

Christian concedes that getting a true handle on Ivanova hasn't been easy, as her character has been notable for her mercurial nature. "Changes? Sure, there have been many changes in this character. In the beginning, I was told to be very stiff, because Susan was brand-new to the station and very aware of the position in which she finds herself. But after the first few episodes, Susan has loosened up and so, suddenly, I was told to relax and show a little more humor.

"With this character, it's a constant challenge to make her interesting, because I have to deal with the audience's expectations of what a female second-in-command should be like. After the first few episodes, I was hearing, 'Well,

she has to thaw out.' That makes me angry because the perception is that, because you're a woman, you have to be soft and demure all the time. Susan can be that but, when she's working, she is a Lt. Commander, and when you're in a position of command, you *can't* be weak and ultrafeminine. There will be time for that once she develops close friendships and starts to trust people."

The actress admits that much of her *Babyon 5* duty is routine genre convention. "There's a lot of the expected technobabble, and I do a lot of glorified parking attendant stuff, like bringing in the ships and making sure everything runs smoothly.

"But there have been episodes where we see Ivanova's emotional side," she says. "We did an episode where my father dies and I have the conflict of remaining professional in my work and yet dealing with my father's death. It's a good episode for Susan, because we see how she keeps things to herself and tries to handle it by herself. It definitely shows what kind of woman she is.

"Another episode deals with Susan's religion. It takes place after her father's death, and she hasn't acknowledged the loss the way the Jewish religion dictates she should. It's a wonderful episode that deals with things that science fiction on television rarely does."

What SF-TV regularly does is shipboard romances, and *Babylon 5* was hardly open for business before reports of an impending love match between Ivanova and Commander Sinclair (Michael O'Hare) began. Christian laughs at the notion before effectively squelching it.

"Not true!" she exclaims emphatically. "The way the military and protocol side of *Babylon 5* is set up, there's no *logical* way you could develop a relationship between those two people. A relationship is being planned between Susan and somebody else in the cast. I can't tell you who, it's all very mysterious."

In the first season of Babylon 5, *Ivanova's boss was Jeff Sinclair (Michael O'Hare), then in command of the space station.*

And of course, romance is unlikely between Ivanova and Sinclair for another more pragmatic reason. O'Hare left the series at the second season's start. Now, Ivanova (who *wasn't* promoted) has to cope with a new commander, John Sheridan (Bruce Boxleitner).

Christian's career in space began, of course, on Earth. Born in Los Angeles and raised in Connecticut, she returned to Southern California, eventually pursuing an acting career.

"I was really confident at an early age," she recalls. "I was in this for life. I knew luck would have a great deal to do with it, but I was really confident that I could work steadily in this business."

Following her acting debut, a small part in *Dallas*, Christian made her genre film bow with *The Hidden*. "That was a very frightening experience for me. It was my first movie and my first scene was a stripping scene. For the record, I played a stripper who gets taken over by the bad alien. It was a great experience and it turned out to be a wonderful film."

A free ticket to Rome was the hook for Christian to play the manager of alien fighters in *Arena*, a film she dismisses as "all right." The actress is even less enthused about her role as a police psychologist in *Maniac Cop 2*. "That was *not* a great experience," she sighs. "It was *very* low budget, we were shooting in New York in the dead of winter and there were no dressing rooms. It was *not* pleasant.

"*Hexed* was something I had high hopes for. The script was very funny. But there were many problems. The film couldn't decide whether it was a comedy or a thriller. Ultimately, it too was not a great film, but I think I'm quite funny in it."

As for *Babylon 5*, Christian appreciates its "take chances/be risky" stance. "There are no rules and what rules there are, you can feel free to break. I also appreciate the opportunity to be a role model for other women; to show them that *anything* is possible."

But how long Christian will have that opportunity is anybody's guess. After all, she replaced an actress and character seen in the pilot. And the series has a five-year story arc already in place, the fates of its characters all locked up in the series' creator's computer.

"I don't even know if I'll be around or even alive after the second season," she relates in a no-nonsense tone. "I don't have a clue. All I know is what I read in the next episode's script.

"But I don't really mind being in limbo. I just do each episode like it's a separate job, and whatever happens happens. I can't do anything to change an already conceived plan. I signed a five-year contract, which implies that my character will be around for the whole time. Unless I screw up or something," she laughs.

But even if Claudia Christian doesn't survive *Babylon 5*'s total run, her "What, me worry?" attitude ultimately proves refreshing.

"This is a good show and it's allowing me to do some quality work. So, yes, I'm grateful for the opportunity, and I would love to stay around until the end and see how my character and her place in the universe unfolds. But whatever happens, I *will* continue to work. I'm not here for a five-year run. I'm here for life."

VOYAGER CAPTAIN

By Ian Spelling

It's very hard work, very challenging work. I'm working on so many different levels as Kathryn Janeway that my vigilance to my craft has been exercised to its fullest capacity. But, by my reckonings, it will remain that way," promises Kate Mulgrew, as she relaxes in her trailer on the Paramount Pictures lot after filming a scene for *Star Trek: Voyager*. "I have to transcend all the normal garbage that gets in the way of good acting. Acting well is my ultimatum, my objective. Janeway, and making her a believable character, is what it's all about."

Captain Kathryn Janeway, of course, proudly commands the starship *Voyager*, which serves as home to a crew of about 140 , and is the focal point of the latest *Star Trek* adventure. In the premiere episode, "The Caretaker," Starfleet has called the *Voyager* and Janeway into action to find a Maquis vessel. Ultimately, an interstellar displacement wave leaves both ships trapped in a far-off region of space, more than 70,000 light years from home, forcing the Starfleet and Maquis crews to bury the hatchet and join forces to find a way back. Janeway remains in the captain's chair, with the former Maquis captain, a Native American named Chakotay (Robert Beltran), as her First Officer. Tom Paris (Robert Duncan McNeill), a former

Starfleet officer turned Maquis renegade who had been languishing in a Starfleet prison, is tapped by Janeway to pilot the *Voyager*.

Also by Janeway's side are Tuvok (Tim Russ), a full Vulcan who serves not just as Tactical/Security officer, but also as Janeway's confidant and the ship's calming influence; Harry Kim (Garrett Wang), a recent Starfleet Academy graduate working as Ops/Communications officer on his first mission; B'Elanna Torres (Roxann Biggs-Dawson), a half-Klingon/half-Human former Maquis whom Janeway chooses over a Starfleet officer to be Chief Engineer; Neelix (Ethan Phillips), an exotic-looking Talaxian whom the Voyager crew picks up and employs as the ship's cook, guide and utility man; Kes (Jennifer Lien), Neelix's assistant and girl friend, who is an Ocampa with a lifespan of only nine years; and, finally, Doc Zimmerman (Robert Picardo), an emergency holographic medical program who becomes the Voyager's sole physician after the ship's doctors are killed.

It's an interesting situation for Janeway, who is definitely a creature of her time. She's a scientist by passion and by legacy—her father was a brilliant scientist as well. But at Starfleet Academy Janeway came to appreciate the regimentation of the military and combined the two disciplines to embark on a respected career in Starfleet. "She has a sense of command that simply *is*, and it's not off-putting. That's true of every real leader we've ever seen," argues the actress. "Leadership-style command has to embrace, but it has to be firm. She's warm, compassionate, very strong. She can be fierce if necessary. She can be abrupt if absolutely necessary, and there will be no nonsense about who is in charge when she is in command.

"However, she's open to suggestions. Many times, you'll see Janeway change a thought or an opinion in mid-sentence because she understands that B'Elanna has an angle on a situation that she missed, or Chakotay says something that makes great sense and she changes her thinking. There's a wonderful flexibility in the middle of this tower of strength. Then, deeply and profoundly, I, as Janeway, am a woman. She's very much a

"There's a chemistry between Paris and Janeway," Mulgrew explains. Her rapport with actor Robert Duncan Neill is equally strong.

creature of the Earth. She is always remembering the past, and her own past. She's left a man she loved and her dog behind. So, Janeway has a conflict that greatly parallels my own life. I love to act, but I also love to be with my children. I love to think. I love intimacy and contact, but acting often takes me away from all of that longer than I care for it to.

"So," she continues, "all of these things are working within Janeway at all times. If I can convey that, which I'm trying hard to do, beneath all the very difficult, highly technical Star Trek language, then I'll be pleased. Ultimately, at its base, is the simplicity of somebody who loves what she does, but, in great part, remains attached to what and where she came from."

Mulgrew sees many challenges ahead for Janeway, the first of which is getting to know and commanding the respect of the Maquis officers who've teamed with the *Voyager* crew. "I think I'll have a lot to do with Paris because there's a chemistry between him and Janeway, and because he's piloting the ship. I like Paris' levity," she notes, "as compared to Janeway's, because it really balances things. He's easy. He's the guy at the bar who says, 'I'll take over that flying.' He'll be a friend to Janeway. And, by the way, that balance is there, too, between Robert and me. Tuvok, interestingly, is the guy I lean on. I lean on Tim Russ instinctively as an actress because he's such a fine actor. I completely believe him as Tuvok and so does Janeway. Tuvok's implacable being relaxes me and I trust him. Janeway senses that beneath that unemotional and, for lack of a better term, impervious facade is a great wealth of knowledge and esteem. So, Paris helps me, Tuvok calms me.

"Chakotay fires me up. It's intense between us, conflicted, which is as it should be. I respect and admire B'Elanna very much. It's the same with Neelix. The guy is marvelous. Not only is he ineffably charming every time he comes into a scene, but he always comes up with some pearl that becomes indispensable to Janeway in whatever the adventure is. He's constantly surprising Janeway.

"I have to tell you, the cast is great, great to a man. Some of them I've come to know a little bit better than others, but that will change," she continues. Robbie McNeill is always jumping into my trailer, bothering me. I love Ethan Phillips. I just think he's terrific. Tim is great. There isn't one bad apple in the bunch."

And what about Janeway's personal relationships? "She has left behind her man, Mark, and her dog," reveals Mulgrew. "It's a situation that saddens her a great deal. She realizes she could be in space for a lifetime and there's no contact possible at this point that we know of, though it may come. Thinking about it doesn't bring her any peace."

To escape from the pressures of command and her interrupted personal life, Janeway spends time in the *Voyager* Holodeck, where she can play a mean game of pool. Further, just as Picard loved to wrap himself in the Holodeck universe of Dixon Hill, Janeway turns to Holonovels for entertainment.

On the voyage homeward, Janeway relies on her Vulcan officer Tuvok (Tim Russ) with his "great wealth of knowledge."

"She has chosen the past, and a basic past, without letting go of her love of discovery. She's still pioneering. There's a robustness to her. She wants to get on a horse and ride. That will be a wonderful way for the audience to see her sadness, her joy, her endless possibilities that simply cannot be expressed on the ship."

The Holonovels, like the series itself, will involve special effects. "It's all very interesting to me. I've never worked with special effects before. It's an integral part of what we do here," she notes, "so I might as well get into it. And that's what I'm doing. I've learned more about camera angles and blue screens and opticals and split screens and all of that, just in the few months I've been here, than you could ever imagine. That's just by listening, watching and observing. I can only help myself by learning."

As for the acting challenges, Mulgrew acknowledges there are many and that, nearly always, they must be dealt with simultaneously. "Let's say I'm having a conversation with Chakotay and I'm making a call about us leaving a certain planet, and that means obliterating the planet. I'm playing three different things at once there," she explains. "I'm letting Chakotay know I'm in command, that I have to overcome him as both the First Officer and as a male who's used to running his own ship. Secondly, I'm making decision based on my background as a military person. Third, I'm overcoming my instinct as a woman to possibly say something nurturing. All of that has to be read by the audience *instantly* in what transpires in that scene. It's not good if I just say 'Look, pal, we're going to do this, and that's it.' You have to see the internal conflict. That's what makes her—I should say that's what *will* make her, if I can do this properly—compelling for people."

A conversation about the strangest thing she has had to do so far as Janeway, not surprisingly, brings Mulgrew back to establishing a believable character. "Everybody is probably telling you about the scene from the pilot in which we're lying naked on a slab with tubes and needles shoved into us," she says, correctly. "I don't find that stuff strange. That was delightful, actually. I rested for 15 minutes. The strangest thing to do, and again, I hark back to it, is endowing the technical language in these long and complicated scenes with a real inner life. That will be an ongoing theme for me, for all of us.

"The perks of it all are that I'm going and running and getting my phaser. Then, I'm lying on the slab and the probe is going in. That's the fun part. The difficult thing is if I've got five minutes with you in a scene, but we're talking about nothing but gravimetric influx centers and plasmic fields, and we've still got to get each other and the audience to understand that and be interested in that. I know I keep saying this, but that's the ongoing challenge, and it's of the utmost importance to me."

Of little importance to Mulgrew is the fact that she stepped into the role of Kathryn Janeway after Genevieve (*Coma*) Bujold decided, after just a day and a half of filming as the then-Elizabeth Janeway, that the demands of weekly, hour-long episodic television were simply too much for her to handle. "I wasn't at all concerned. This is a funny thing about me and I hope it doesn't smack of arrogance. But I'm used to shot-out-of-the-cannon situations working in my favor," explains Mulgrew, who admits that her first audition for the part wasn't particularly memorable.

"I'm the second oldest of eight children. I always had to move quickly and incisively growing up. As a young actress in New York City, it served me well. It wasn't that I was fearless, but I loved the challenge of being asked, 'Can you do this tomorrow, because it's virtually impossible?' I always want to say that I can try. So, I was terribly excited to get to audition again and to have this opportunity. Let me constantly remind you that the standards I've set for myself are very high. Everyone expects a lot from me and I want to give it to them."

As soon as Mulgrew won the role, she began to immerse herself in the world of *Star Trek*, watching old episodes and

turning to one of her best friends, John de Lancie, well known to *Trek* fans as the all-powerful Q, for advice. "I was very aware of *Star Trek*. John and I would watch his episodes of *Next Generation*, then we would talk about them," she remembers. "There seemed to be a high level of writing and a real elevated level of professionalism on the show. When I got the job, they sent me a dozen or so tapes of the show and I was very impressed. I could see how people could get so totally addicted to it. The language alone is extraordinary. These writers sit in a room and come up with it and I couldn't dream up such stuff if my life depended on it. Then, they have the interpersonal stuff going and there's an emotional level, too. It's very, very good work."

It's mentioned to Mulgrew that Marina Sirtis and Gates McFadden often voiced distress over how 20th Century men wrote for 24th-Century women, particularly early on, and that their lobbying for better dialogue and, frankly, more to do on *Next Generation* eventually paid off not just for them, but for Terry Farrell and Nana Visitor on *Deep Space Nine* as well.

Mulgrew's eyes narrow. It's clear she has gotten the point, but feels it's a case of mixing apples and oranges. "We're talking about the captain in this instance. That's the ultimate. It really can't be compared to *any* other kind of role. The captain is almost without gender regarding substance," she stresses. "Anybody in that role, if the captain is the lead role, will be given, or had better be given, substantive dialogue: man, woman or alien.

"Will it be a pioneering gesture regarding the writers, the producers and all of that? Absolutely. But I still argue that Janeway, as the captain, stands apart as a role in a way that doesn't bleed into 'Will this help women?' For me to speak about it as such would be presumptuous, I think, at this point. What we're doing is great. It's terribly courageous of them and it's certainly appropriate. Gene Roddenberry would approve of this. We're looking into the future here, and this would be right at that time. Anyway, I don't really subscribe to what those other ladies have said because it has never really been my experience, *Star Trek* or otherwise. Beautiful writers write beautifully, regardless."

Certainly, there will be countless women, young and old, who will be thrilled to see a woman in the captain's chair on a *Star Trek* series, and many of them will be scribbling and inputting letters to this science-fiction heroine, in which they'll call her a role model and an inspiration and ask for everything from autographs to advice. What will Mulgrew do when the envelopes start pouring in? "I don't know," she responds. "What am I going to do? Am I going to write back? I would thank them for taking the time to write me an acknowledgement of this role and whatever they think I bring to it. It takes time, energy and a stamp to write me. Then, I would probably encourage them to be bold in life and tell them that dreams do come true and that you must aspire to the greatest possible thing."

The greatest possible thing to which Mulgrew has always aspired is success as an actor. By age 12, growing up in Iowa, a place where actresses "are not exactly nurtured," she knew the life of a thespian was for her. Fortunately, her parents supported her efforts as did a teacher who was a nun. "I was encouraged, fiercely encouraged by the people who loved me. I

For Janeway, getting to know strange alien life forms begins on her own ship—with Neelix (Ethan Phillips).

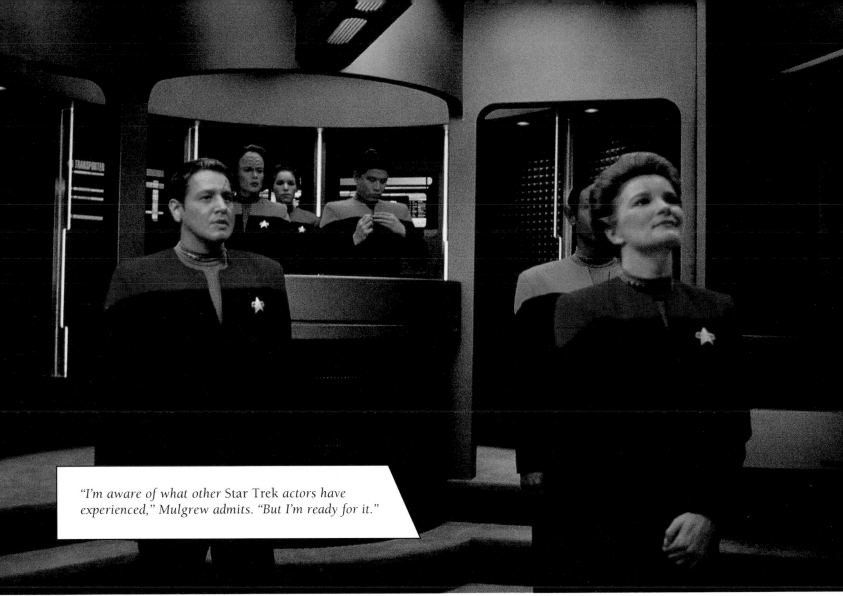

"*I'm aware of what other* Star Trek *actors have experienced,*" Mulgrew admits. "*But I'm ready for it.*"

came home one day and said to my mother, 'I read this poem in class today and everybody was crying and I just adored what I did. I loved the reaction and I want to do it again,' " she remembers. "And my mother said, 'Well, if you're serious, we'll see in a year's time.' I got very serious and started to study when I was 13. It was just in the blood."

A move to Manhattan at age 17 led to the young Mulgrew being accepted into both New York University and the Stella Adler Conservatory, a respected acting school. She dropped out of NYU after her junior year to pursue a career and promptly proceeded to land, simultaneously, the roles of Emily in an American Shakespeare Festival production of *Our Town* and Mary Ryan on the soap opera *Ryan's Hope*.

Subsequent work included the films *A Stranger is Watching, Remo Williams: The Adventure Begins* and *Throw Momma from the Train*, while, on television, Mulgrew made guest appearances on such series as *Cheers* and *Murphy Brown*, and had lead roles in *Mrs. Columbo, Heartbeat* and *Man of the People*.

"My favorites have been my theater work, almost all of it," says Mulgrew, reflecting on her credits thus far.

"The real highlight of acting for me is my absolute love of the craft. I'm one of the very few actors you will probably ever talk to who has awakened every single day of her life and not regretted for one instant that acting was her choice. It has been my passion all my life, and I think that is just a gift from God."

One of her credits of interest to genre fans is *Remo Williams,* an action-adventure based on the Destroyer novels by Richard Sapir and Warren Murphy, in which she co-starred opposite Fred Ward as Remo Williams and Joel Grey, behind a convincing layer of makeup, as the soap opera-addicted Korean Sinanju master Chiun. "I liked that. It was fun," says Mulgrew, laughing. "My baby was just born, so I had two little kids at home and I was in Mexico forever filming that. It was a good film, but I wanted it to be better. It was supposed to be the first of a series, but the studio didn't know what to do with it and it really wasn't quite good enough to launch a series of films."

And now there is *Voyager,* which means a unique kind of stardom, convention appearances, and all sorts of *Trek*-related paraphernalia—from action figures to posters and from CD-ROM games to key chains—all bearing Mulgrew's image. "I've heard how big all of this is. I'm aware of what previous *Star Trek* actors have experienced," she admits. "I somehow think it won't actually happen until after we premiere. That's good. I need this time. But I'm ready for it. Sure, I'm ready. It'll be big, then at some point, it will end. Hopefully, I will have done the right thing, the best thing, by doing *Voyager*. I'm very excited by it.

"Janeway is the captain and she has everywhere to go as a character. I would like to take her down into the deepest depths of hell and bring her up again. I would like to see her weeping. I would like to see her out of control, but only for a while. I would like to see her make calls everyone else is opposed to. I would like to see her experience every shade, color and emotion. All of it.

"And," concludes Kate Mulgrew, "I'm sure she will."

QUEEN OF SCREAMS

By Roy Kinnard

It's an incredible movie moment as the beautiful Ann Darrow, imprisoned and bound before a great door, awaits her dread fate. Drums pound. The natives chant. Then, suddenly, *he* is there.

Ann Darrow stares up and into the face of Kong. She screams. Beauty has met her beast.

For Fay Wray, the star of the landmark 1933 film *King Kong*, it's a moment to remember. She still recalls all that screaming.

"The first time I saw *King Kong*, I was distressed by how much screaming there was in it," she says. "It seemed too much to me, and I realized only later that a lot of screaming was necessary in order to give life to the little animated figure of me in Kong's hand, and without the screaming, it *wouldn't* have seemed alive. These essentially had to be long shots, but still, *all* of that screaming seemed overdone to me at the time."

Screaming aside, getting cast in the movie was relatively easy for Wray. "I had done a film called *The Four Feathers* with [producer] Merian C. Cooper, and so when he was preparing *King Kong*, he thought of me, and asked me to come to the studio and talk about it. It was very simple—he just wanted me to do it.

"Merian Cooper was one of the most unusual men ever to work in films, and he was one of the most unusual characters in my life. He had a background that was astonishing. Born in Florida, he was a real Southern gentleman and had a chivalrous attitude toward women. He had graduated from the Naval Academy, and after he left the Navy, he decided to become a journalist. During the First World War, Cooper went to Persia. He was shot down and taken prisoner by the Russians, but then escaped. He met [fellow *Kong* collaborator] Ernest Schoedsack, who was driving an ambulance. They met on a station platform, and they just hit it off, became good friends—and that's when they went off to make pictures together in faraway places. Pretty colorful, right? Cooper liked the wilderness and animals, and yet was a very intelligent, social person. But he really liked faraway places better than civilization. He was fascinating; I looked upon him as a kind of father figure."

Over the past 60 years, Wray has done a great deal of talking about *Kong*—in numerous print and TV interviews, personal appearances at film festivals, retrospectives and even at New York City's Empire State Building (which she had *never* visited in real life until decades after the movie's release). She has also penned an autobiography, *On the Other Hand: A Life Story* (St. Martin's Press, 1989). Still, the questions remain.

Wray says that the ones she's asked most often about *King Kong* are " 'How did they *do* it?' 'Was that a big animal?' 'Was it a man in a suit?' And of course the answer to those questions is, 'No, that was an 18-inch tall figure.' Then the question follows, 'Well, how did they get pictures of you in an 18-inch tall figure's hand?' And so I explain about the full-sized Kong hand,

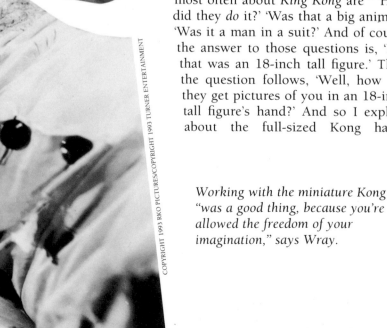

Working with the miniature Kong "was a good thing, because you're allowed the freedom of your imagination," says Wray.

and how once I was secure in it, with the fingers pressed tightly around me, they photographed me quite separately from anything else.

"There were special problems just in the way it was done. Having to just imagine Kong instead of having anyone or anything to look at. That was a good thing, because you're allowed the freedom of your imagination, but it was tough in a way, too. I don't see it that way; thought it was a performance that I just did. I don't think in terms of the difficulties."

Unfortunately, Wray, one of the very first science-fiction heroines, had almost no personal contact with Willis O'Brien, the special FX genius who made her 18-inch tall leading man so alive. "He came on the set one day, but didn't mingle. I just remember *seeing* him on the set. He was such a gifted man."

Her *King Kong* co-stars, the human ones, were Bruce Cabot and Robert Armstrong. "Bruce was fine. He was OK, very straightforward," Wray notes. "Robert Armstrong, too, was very straightforward and *very* professional."

The film they made together still fascinates and frightens audiences today. It's a legacy the actress never expected. "Of course not," Wray declares. "Whenever one makes a film, you want it to be good, but I don't think anyone ever predicts such a sustained life for a film. I really wasn't thinking that way at all. We couldn't have imagined that, and it's kind of wonderful that *King Kong* has endured."

Of *King Kong*'s "sister" production, *The Most Dangerous Game*, filmed on many of the same sets during a break in *Kong*'s production, Wray recalls, "I haven't seen that in a long time, but I thought it was a very interesting story, with a wonderfully ironic twist—that humans should hunt each other instead of animals. Merian Cooper always had a different concept of making films, and I trusted him."

In 1932–33, Wray co-starred with Lionel Atwill in a trio of horror films. *Doctor X* (1932) and *Mystery of the Wax Museum* (1933) were both shot in the two-strip Technicolor process by famed Warner Bros. director Michael Curtiz (later known for *The Adventures of Robin Hood* and *Casablanca*), while *The Vampire Bat* (Majestic, 1933) was a poverty-row effort directed by Frank Strayer. Of her triple stint with Atwill, Wray observes, "Lionel was a very professional person, very proper. I saw *Doctor X* in Minneapolis just a couple of years ago. I thought it was paced a little too fast, and everyone talked too fast, that would

---

"*King Kong* has had a lovely impact," notes Wray, looking down from atop the Empire State Building. "I'm happy to know that."

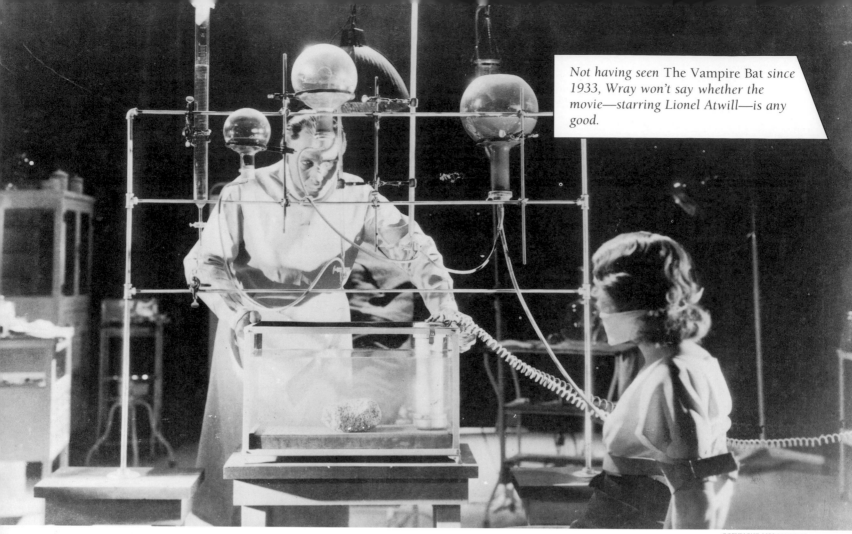

Not having seen The Vampire Bat *since 1933, Wray won't say whether the movie—starring Lionel Atwill—is any good.*

be a criticism of it. During filming, I didn't have many personal conversations with [leading man] Lee Tracy, but he was just like you see him on the screen—kind of casual, easy-going and very snappy.

"*Mystery of the Wax Museum* had certain strengths. Originally, it was very harsh color-wise. Then, I saw the film recently, restored by UCLA, and I thought they did a *beautiful* job. The color had a kind of antique look that took away the harshness I remember when I saw it in preview, after we finished making it. The colors in the restoration were very mellow, and it was fascinating. The problem at that time [1933] with color was that they needed so much light in order to photograph that it was just devastating. It was really, really hot, and that was tough.

"Michael Curtiz—well, he was a *very* able director, very efficient, but very unemotional, almost like a machine. He didn't give detailed direction; you just knew the scene had to be done and so you did it."

Two other 1930s horror movies found her on the scene for screams. "*Black Moon* [Columbia, 1934] is a film that I've almost erased from my consciousness," Wray admits. "I've *never* seen it. I've seen stills of it, and I thought they were quite interesting.

"*The Clairvoyant* [British, 1935, a.k.a. *The Evil Mind*] was a very interesting story. [Co-star] Claude Rains was a fine actor. It wasn't just a 'strange' movie, but had a lot of character development. Claude played a fake mindreader, who then began to believe in himself and make predictions that came true. He performed that so well."

After a lengthy retirement to family life that kept her off movie screens for most of the '40s, Wray returned to film in character roles a decade later, and also worked in television, even appearing in the *Alfred Hitchcock Presents* episodes "The Morning After" and the Hitchcock-directed Roald Dahl tale "A Dip in the Pool."

"Hitchcock was *very* pleasant," she recalls. "He had such a charming sense of humor, and I actually knew him as a friend. It was just a very easy, splendid kind of character role. He was very efficient, knew everything that was happening and wasn't the least bit sloppy; he was a *very* organized man. I had a lot of respect for his ability."

In more recent years, Wray has all but retired from acting. Her last role was a memorable turn in the acclaimed 1980 TV movie *Gideon's Trumpet*.

Everything Wray has done stands in the shadow of *King Kong* and its incredible popularity. "As time goes on, I feel so pleased that the film is really appreciated. I'm certain it has been shown in every country in the world, and that gives me a good feeling; I'm happy to know that it has had that broad reception. *King Kong* has had a lovely impact. I didn't realize for the first 10 years after it was first released *how much* it was appreciated," she announces. "And then, as time has gone by, *King Kong* seems to have even grown in appeal, so I am very glad—that just makes me feel good."

Now, more than 60 years later, *King Kong* continues to rule the imagination of fans everywhere. And Fay Wray is still Queen of Screams. Do fans ever ask her for a sample, a little bit of high-pitched terror, for just a scream?

"Little children, children of my friends did, long ago. That's long past, thank goodness," she explains. "They used to ask, 'Would you *scream* for us, please?'" And she laughs.

40

WOMAN OF THE FORBIDDEN PLANET

By Tom Weaver

It's one of the indelible images of the 1950s: Against a backdrop of astral blackness and ringed planets, a fearsome-looking robot looms. Lying unconscious in this metal monster's arms is a mini skirted girl with long ash-blond hair (and longer legs). Every science fiction fan worth his salt knows that this is the emblem for *Forbidden Planet*, MGM's one major contribution to the 1950s' SF boom, and that the "fearsome" mechanical man is actually the astounding Robby the Robot, "poster boy" for '50s SF. Does that make Anne Francis SF fans' favorite pin-up girl?

"I got that part because I was under contract to MGM and I had good legs," the actress blurts out with no hesitation, "and still *do*, I might add.

"When I was doing *Forbidden Planet*, it seemed quite obvious that the Id was similar to what one in metaphysics would call the mass subconscious, and that what we put into this mass subconscious in our thinking *comes back*. Much as it says in the Bible, 'That which I have feared the most has come upon me.' So, at that time, it didn't seem dumb to me that the collective thinking could create a monster. It *still* doesn't seem dumb to me that our collective thinking is creating monsters—like nuclear bombs and everything else. At the time, the story made sense enough to me."

That kind of pro-found evaluation of *Forbidden Planet* might sound odd coming from some other '50s ingenue, but not from the actress whose list of credits includes *Forbidden Planet* as only *one* of many memorable titles. Born in Ossining, New York, Francis began her amazing career when she was six months old, posing for calendar photos. Before she was five, she was a fashion model whose image appeared in many national magazines; she made her television debut on an NBC Christmas show in 1939; and she was on Broadway at age 11, playing Gertrude Lawrence as a child in the stage hit *Lady in the Dark*. More than 3,000 radio appearances during the 1940s earned the blue-eyed trouper the nickname "The Little Queen of Soap Operas."

In the early '50s, Francis went to Hollywood again, landing a berth as a contract player at 20th Century Fox. In December

COPYRIGHT 1956 MGM

Filming Forbidden Planet *was fun for Anne Francis. She "was madly in love with" co-star Leslie Nielson.*

One of several characters anxious to teach the "facts of life" to the naive girl, Jack Kelly also courted Francis' Altaira.

1953, she played her first SF film lead in the Lenny Bruce-scripted SF/comedy *The Rocket Man* (shooting title: *The Kid from Outer Space*), but (like co-stars John Agar and Beverly Garland) she remembers little of the experience. Far better and more memorable days awaited her once she changed studios and became part of the MGM "family" where she appeared in the 1955 classics *Blackboard Jungle* and *Bad Day at Black Rock*.

What might have been her *least* challenging MGM role has, of course, become her best-known, as Francis portrayed Altaira, the unworldly daughter of space pioneer Walter Pidgeon, in the studio's *Forbidden Planet*. Playing the naive character with the scene-stealing legs required "no great preparation on my part: I wasn't that worldly-wise at that point myself! I remember that there were some costumes that they decided were too revealing. One was a silver lamé jumpsuit with silver boots—just absolutely gorgeous. It's rumored that [studio production head] Dore Schary's wife Miriam nixed it, saying that it was just too sexy, too extreme. It covered me from head to toe, along with the silver boots that matched this lamé suit. Kind of shows you how far we've come since then."

Remembering her *Planet* co-stars, Francis smiles. "Walter Pidgeon loved to recite dirty limericks—he was a wonderful gentleman in every way, except for his proclivity for dirty limericks! Which were really *very* funny—they were sort of 'the thing' back then.

"And Leslie Nielsen, I was *madly* in love with! Les was a very gentle, kind, terrific guy, just as he is today. He had a great sense of humor: today it has become more extreme than it was when I worked with him in those days," she laughs. "But Les

has a wonderful basic outlook on life, and he doesn't take himself seriously. Or, if he *does*, it's not noticeable on the outside."

What about Robby the Robot? "Robby got drunk one day at noon and his innards [actor Frankie Darro] were promptly replaced!" Francis recalls, letting out another laugh. "He almost took a full nosedive—if three grips hadn't grabbed him in time. Robby was the most expensive 'actor' on the picture—the *outer* Robby, not the inner! The facade was worth much more than *any* of the actors; the actors could have been replaced, but Robby would have been a terrible expense. Robby was really the star of the show, so the young man who was working him from the inside was replaced one afternoon after a five martini lunch. Drunken robots are not to be countenanced!"

The hardest part of *Forbidden Planet*, Francis adds, was "reacting to things that weren't there. Disney's people did all of the special FX, the cartooning of the monster and all those things. That was all post-production. We were racing through the film, running away from things we had to imagine at all times. It was a matter of trying to grade our fear from one scene to another, from apprehension to," she laughs, "horrific extremes of facial expressions! That was the film's major challenge for *all* of us.

"Fred Wilcox, the director, was fine, but his direction was, 'Look scared. Look *more* scared.' It wasn't an in-depth character study. I was the ingenue. It was pretty well-defined, who each of us was. It was a science-fiction fairy tale, and I was the sleeping princess—no more, no less. I was awakened by the prince who landed in his flying saucer. I don't think anything more could be made of it; that's what the story was and there really wasn't much else to do. Yes, it's condescending, but that's what the story was. It's still going on today.

"Maybe women's roles have matured to a certain point," she adds, "except that I think that many films are still playing the sex game. Instead of really having much 'growth' with the women, their idea of 'feminine freedom' is that *now*, one takes off more clothes. *That's* 'feminine freedom.' I don't think there's that much more respect for women [in films] now than there was then. The attitude that women don't have much to offer society. But that has gone on for centuries."

Regarding *Forbidden Planet*'s enduring appeal, Francis admits, "At the time, I don't think that any of us were really aware of the fact that it was going to turn into a longtime cult film, probably much, much stronger today than it was then. *Forbidden Planet* just had a life of its own."

Her favorite scene in the film? "Probably any scene where I kissed Les Nielsen, 'cause I had that terrible crush on him! And if Les does another *Naked Gun* movie, I think it would be wonderful fun for me to run through in the background with the lion—in the same outfit!"

Freelancing after leaving MGM at her own request, Francis turned up in the occasional movie, like the SF thrillers *The Satan Bug* and *Brainstorm*. But she worked more steadily in television where (among many other series) she acted in *Alfred Hitchcock Presents*, *The Man From U.N.C.L.E.*, *The Invaders* and, perhaps most notably, *The Twilight Zone* (the memorable "The After Hours" episode).

"Rod Serling was a wonderful man—a *brilliant* man, with a great sense of humor. That was back in the days when we rehearsed the show for a full week before we shot it, so we knew every shot that was going to be done. It was wonderful to do that."

Some fans also know Francis from her one-year run as TV's *Honey West*, a James Bond-ish private detective (complete with futuristic communicators and spy equipment). "*Honey West* was fun to do, because we had such wonderful character actors on the show—I really enjoyed it for that reason. I also loved the physical activity involved. I studied Karate for the show and worked out to get in shape for it."

In the '70s and '80s, her career took on yet more diversity, with Francis trying directing ("I didn't *try*; I *did* direct!") and also turning authoress. Her short film *Gemini Rising* (1970), about rodeo riders, has been seen on PBS, and her "spiritual exposé" *Voices from Home: An Inner Journey* was published in 1982.

She realizes that, for many people, she'll always be best remembered as the science-fiction heroine of *Forbidden Planet*, but she takes the realistic stance that "I don't have much to say about that, really. It's OK with me because I acccept *life* as 'OK.' To make it 'un-OK' would be spending time in a mood or an attitude that's not very beneficial."

According to Anne Francis, there is no "down side" to being a cult actress. "I have fun: I sign posters and things that are sent to me. I answer letters from those who seem most sincere. Years ago, I got a postcard which was just *crammed* with writing about how wonderful, how terrific, how great I was. 'Would it be possible, do you think, that I could ever meet you? I would love to marry you!' was all squeezed onto the card in tiny little letters. Then at the bottom, it said, 'P.S.: If you're not interested, would you send this to Debbie Reynolds?' "

"*Robby the Robot was the most expensive 'actor' in the picture,*" Francis notes.

SPACE MOM

By Tom Weaver and Steve Swires

June Lockhart, an actress for more than half-a-century, is most famous for the mothers she played down on Earth in TV's *Lassie* and somewhere out there *Lost in Space*.

As Maureen Robinson, *Lost in Space*'s understanding, brow-knitting mom, Lockhart could show all the motherly concern she could muster—but none of the wifely affection. "Guy Williams [as her husband] and I *did* have scenes of intimacy in the beginning. Great affection was shown, hand-holding and kisses—in the pilot, it's all there. But the word came down from CBS that we were not to touch each other because, they said, it embarrassed children watching at home to see the parents kissing. Well, we couldn't believe it. Guy and I had put in all these little things to try and give this family a

warmth like that—being demonstrably affectionate was always something I was raised with."

Her parents were Gene Lockhart (1891–1957), the veteran vaudeville and stage actor and writer, and actress Kathleen (1894–1978). Born in New York City, only-child June made her professional debut at age eight in a Metropolitan Opera production of *Peter Ibbetson*, playing Mimsey in the dream sequence. In the mid-30s, the Lockharts relocated to California, where father Gene enjoyed a long career as one of the screen's great character actors. June made her screen debut in MGM's 1938 version of Charles Dickens' *A Christmas Carol*, playing—appropriately enough—the daughter of stars Gene and Kathleen Lockhart.

Eventually, June Lockhart carved a career as an actress, appearing in such films as *Sergeant York*, *Meet Me in St. Louis* and *She-Wolf of London* (as a woebegone lass convinced she's a lycanthrope). She became an accomplished Broadway actress (winning a Tony), a prolific veteran of 1950s live TV drama and even a journalist (who still occasionally attends White House press briefings). Her work on *Lassie* followed.

It was a guest spot on *Voyage to the Bottom of the Sea* which led to Lockhart's *other* most famous TV role. Acting in the episode "The Ghost of Moby Dick," she met veteran producer Irwin Allen. "I had *not* met him before. I was doing that *Voyage* guest appearance in August or September [1964], and on the second day, Irwin saw the rushes of the *first* day. He came down and found me and said, 'We're doing a series called *Space Family Robinson*. Would you like to do another series?' I said yes, and so he gave me the script and I called my agent and said, 'This looks interesting.' So, we did it."

Rechristened *Lost in Space*, the original series pilot—at that time one of the most expensive in TV history (more than $600,000)—began shooting January 6, 1965 on the 20th Century Fox Westwood lot. Newcomers to this planet will need to know that it starred Guy Williams as astrophysicist John Robinson and Lockhart as his biochemist wife Maureen; accompanied by their children Judy (Marta Kristen), Penny (Angela Cartwright) and Will (Bill Mumy) and by Dr. Don West (Mark Goddard), the space pioneers set out aboard the *Gemini 12* to colonize the planet Alpha Centauri, only to be sidetracked by a meteor storm which sends them into the uncharted depths of outer space.

Before the series reached the airwaves, extensive changes were made, including the addition of Jonathan Harris as the saboteur caught aboard the spacecraft (renamed *Jupiter 2*) just before liftoff. Convoluted pilots and intricate special FX often caused delays.

"The hours were very very long. And there *was* a lot of physical stuff—there was less of that to do later in the run, because the storyline changed, but yes, the pilot was *very* physical, and and all the flying on wires—*that* was an experience! And it was very hot, of course, in those silver lamé suits. However, we just accepted it all and did the job. We had some very good directors on *Lost in Space* that first season, but they usually only did one or two shows, and then probably went to a halfway house!" she laughs.

A new title wasn't the only change instituted once the series started shooting. The expensively

Once Lost in Space, *June Lockhart has always had her feet on the ground.*

Early scenes of intimacy between the Robinsons were deep-sixed by network execs who felt children would be embarrassed by them.

produced pilot didn't air in its original form. "What happened was that the pilot had too many climaxes in it," Lockhart discloses. "We were caught in a whirlpool and frozen, then we saw a one-eyed giant, then we crash-landed. These sequences were cut up and became the climaxes of the first *five* episodes. We had to shoot new scenes leading up to these climaxes which we had already shot. All the pilot's footage was eventually aired."

As the matriarch of a family stranded in space, Lockhart faced many unique acting problems peculiar to science-fiction heroes and heroines. Although she looks back with humor at the rigors of fantasy filming, the actual work experience wasn't always enjoyable. "The costumes were *unbearably* hot." she complains. "They were really racing car drivers' fireproof aluminum suits. We had to wear them because there was no fabric which had the same look. And they were so tight, we couldn't sit down in them. When we moved, we were all *very* stiff-legged.

"In order to rest between shots, I had to hold somebody's hand and be lowered back onto a cot, and then be helped to stand up. Otherwise, I couldn't get my legs under me. Underneath, we wore body stockings, so we could drop the tops down and be comfortable—at least from the waist up. Finally, in the third season, we wore silver jerseys made of mylar. Unfortunately, that hadn't been invented in time for the first two seasons."

Lockhart easily coped with the challenges of filming reaction shots to special FX which weren't added until post-production on *Lost in Space*. "You could pretend *anything* while doing such a scene," she points out. "You just dip into your little bag of reactions and pretend you're in peril. When I was doing *Lassie*, for example, I knew there actually *wasn't* a bear in the tree, but I did have to protect the kid and the dog.

"It's really just a game. If you go overboard with your own reaction, the audience has nothing to be frightened about seeing. If you carry on too much, you remove their involvement. I don't follow any formula for filming reaction shots, other than 'Don't smile until the director yells 'Cut!' "

Nevertheless, in the opinion of many fans, *Lost in Space* took a somewhat juvenile approach to science fiction. "Perhaps that's what it evolved into being," Lockhart concedes. "Initially, though, the show was meant to be like *Swiss Family Robinson*, except in space. It was supposed to deal with the problems of a family and the extraordinary experiences they had while surviving in space. But, certainly, it *did* change, becoming more of a comedy."

45

Eventually, the series shifted its dramatic emphasis from the Robinsons to the comedic villainy of Dr. Smith (Jonathan Harris, right).

the set, it was just *amazing*—all that great silver hardware and lights blinking and things going on up and down. It was really quite wonderful."

Given her dissatisfaction with her reduced participation, Lockhart wasn't especially disappointed when the series was cancelled in 1968, after its third season. "I thought we had rung as many changes as we could on the boy, the doctor and the robot in space. However, had the series been renewed for a fourth season, I would have stayed with it. In the long run, I was still the star of the show for three years. Nobody knew from week to week how many lines I had. I had been in the business for a few years before *Lost in Space*, and I knew I would work after *Lost in Space*."

Retirement—or even just the thought of it—is apparently nowhere on the horizon for the actress, who has continued to make movies and TV guest shots since *Lost in Space* was grounded. She has no regrets. "I *never* had a desire to be famous. I never had that driving force—gotta act, gotta get out there! It has just unfolded *so* naturally in my life. The agonies that some people go through, waiting for the phone to ring, wanting that great public success, hasn't been part of my makeup—because of what I saw my parents do, and what their concerns were with *life* as it should be lived."

She has watched her own daughters grow, and now enjoys seeing her daughter Anne's acting career develop. "She was Sheba in *Battlestar Galactica*. She's a very good actress, and has great potential still."

Mother and daughter both appeared in 1986's *Troll*, with Anne playing the younger version of her white-wigged mother. The *Gremlins*-like film didn't get a great reception from fans, but Lockhart—who *swears* in the movie (gasp!)—also swears by the experience. "*Troll*—God, I had the best time! We shot it in Italy, and on days when we weren't working, they made all the arrangements for the most fabulous sightseeing—off to Rome, Florence, Venice. Lordy me, it was wonderful, and I would go again in a New York minute!"

Obviously, the *real* June Lockhart is a very different person from many of the poised, serene, housebound women that she has played in her long career. A *TV Guide* article once called her a "happy nut," a description that might ruffle many actresses, but she just laughs it off. "Well, I don't know if *nut* is quite the word now, because nut may have a different connotation these days than it did years ago, when that was written. But I certainly am . . . *outrageous!* One of my greatest compliments in life was when Annie called me an eccentric, and I shouted, 'Hallelujah! I've been waiting for eccentric-hood all my life!' She didn't mean it as a compliment at all, but *by God*, it was neat. *Who wouldn't want to be an original?*"

The addition of Harris (after the pilot's shooting) to the cast helped take the series in a whole new direction; Lockhart isn't certain whether the show would have been more successful had it stayed "serious" rather than going the "camp" route. "I don't know—it's hard to say but *that* is what they chose to do with the show, to make it a comedy show about an old man [Harris] and a little boy [Mumy] in space. There's still a lot of unmined area there, to have a *real* show about a family colonizing a new planet. That certainly would have been a different show! Would it have run as long, or *longer*, I don't know."

Her role diminished in size as the series concentrated more on the misadventures of Harris and Mumy (and the Robot, played by Bob May), but Lockhart wasn't disappointed by the change. "It took a while to realize that was the direction they were going in. But I certainly didn't agitate to leave the show, I believe in contracts, and certainly was happy to stay until its finish." Hers was also the only character which was never once the centerpiece of an episode. "Yes, I think that's right, and, you know, that *never* occurred to me before. That shows you where my ego is, I guess!"

Even if *Lost in Space* did represent long hours and an undemanding role, there were plenty of rewards, like the opportunity to bring her daughters Anne Kathleen (born 1953) and June Elizabeth (1955) to the set. "But we *all* loved

BRIDE OF THE FLY

By Anthony Timpone and Carr D'Angelo

Acting alongside a 185-pound mutated man-insect probably isn't the easiest way for an actress to earn a living. But for Geena Davis, the romantic lead in David Cronenberg's acclaimed update of *The Fly*, the part was too good to let a little unpleasantness spoil things.

"I have a pretty strong stomach," explains Davis. "I never turn away when I watch horror movies, and I didn't walk away from what went on during *The Fly*. When you're behind the scenes, it all looks fake. When Jeff Goldblum [her co-star] throws up though, it's pretty disgusting. Watching him vomit was certainly worse than blood squirting or eyes popping out."

In *The Fly*, Davis plays Veronica Quaife, a magazine journalist who interviews Seth Brundle (Goldblum), an eccentric scientist experimenting with transmitting matter from one place to another. The two fall in love, but a molecular mix-up occurs in the experiment. Quaife tries to keep cool while her man slowly metamorphosizes into the title creature. For this offbeat relationship movie, Davis had to learn to believably react to Chris (*Gremlins*) Walas' amazing *Fly* prosthetics that covered Goldblum in pounds of foam rubber.

"Fortunately, Jeff only turns into the *Fly* about halfway through the movie," Davis laughs, "and then not even totally. He goes through a gradual change. In the first part of the picture, he's a real person. But it is somewhat unusual having to think about how to respond in a situation like that. It's not something you come across every day.

"On *The Fly*, Jeff is extraordinary," comments the soft-spoken actress, "even in full suit and makeup. It's amazing how much acting comes through and how he portrays any kind of emotion, especially with his face. You can read his entire emotions through all that makeup. It's a combination of his terrific talent as well as the makeup artist's skill."

"I see The Fly *as a tragic love story,"* Davis explains, the tale of a woman and her Brundlefly.

COPYRIGHT 1986 20TH CENTURY FOX FILM CORP.

"I just saw the first *Fly* recently," Davis explains. "The original story is very different from ours, and all that remains is the germ of the idea—a scientist fusing with a fly—but even that's different in the new version. Any movie from that period seems a little hokey today, but I like the original *Fly*."

Like the fondly remembered science-fiction heroines of the past from Fay Wray onward, one thing that Davis gets to do a great deal of in *The Fly* is scream and scream again. Her vocal histrionics led to one particularly amusing incident while the production went on location in Toronto.

"We shot a scene where we were in an actual hospital operating room," she remembers with a chuckle, "where I'm giving birth and screaming very loudly. I could imagine what the real patients must have thought not knowing a movie was being shot: 'Who is being tortured?' It was like going to a dentist and the patient inside is screaming before it's your turn."

Before learning to yell her lungs out in Canadian delivery rooms, Davis studied the piano, flute and organ during a quiet childhood. She became a top model and TV commercial figure. Eventually, roles on the sitcoms *Buffalo Bill* and *Sara* led to movies like *Fletch*, *Tootsie* and *Transylvania 6-5000* in which she played an oversexed vampiress.

Moving on to more serious fare with *The Fly*, Davis explains that as an actress, she deals with comedy in the same manner she handles a dramatic role. "I approach acting from the same vantage point all the time, whether it's comedy or drama. You just make the situation and people real, no matter what."

That's even true when your character isn't much of a live one, as Davis emphasized in *Beetlejuice*. "We're the most normal people in the movie, even though we're dead. That's the most unique thing about us," she says. Barbara (Davis) and Adam Maitland (Alec Baldwin) are a young married couple who depart this mortal coil early on in the film ("Around page 10," Davis laughs. "It's crash, we're dead."). Expecting to cosmically cocoon in their haunted homestead for the next century or so, the ghostly Maitlands' plans are upset when a family of madcap Manhattanites—Jeffrey Jones, Catherine O'Hara and Winona Ryder—invade the premises.

"It's the people who move in who are weird and scary and are scaring *us*," Davis explains. "So, we're trying to figure out how to be ghosts. We're inept ghosts. How do you do it? Do you say, 'Boo!'? We've never done it before and can't quite figure it out. At one point, we equate it to stereo instructions—it's too complicated.

"The funny thing about *Beetlejuice* is that we don't behave in any way as if we're dead. It seems to be just like being alive. Much of the humor comes from us sticking to our way of operating even though we're going to these weird places and meeting weird people. In the afterlife, everybody seems distasteful and scary to us. Tim Burton says once that it's like riding on the subway. You're not freaking out, but you're thinking, 'Where did these people come from? They're so unattractive.' So, we relate to things exactly as we would have if we were alive."

To maintain the delicate balance between the story's fantasy aspects and its comedic moments, special care was taken with special FX. "With the way the effects were worked in *Beetle-*

Originally, it wasn't the special makeup FX that attracted Davis to this $15 million SF project, but the script by Charles Edward Pogue and David Cronenberg. "Jeff had the part first," she recalls, "and I read his script. I told him, 'Wow! This is a great script and something I would *like* to do, too. There's a great part in it for me.' It's very intelligent and not really like a horror movie, though it has those elements and FX which are integral to the plot. There's nothing gratuitous about *The Fly*, no extra gore. The plot is classy and logical."

Additionally, *The Fly* presented another first for the Massachusetts-born former model. "It's obviously the biggest part I've ever had in a film," notes Davis. "Veronica is a demanding part. I get to go through several changes myself—*emotionally*, that is. It's exciting to evolve as a character during a limited time span. I start out as a totally different person than the one I end up as. In the beginning, I'm self-confident, somewhat cocky, sarcastic and sure of myself. When all hell breaks loose, though, Veronica is terribly affected by it all.

"I see *The Fly* as a tragic love story," she confesses. "It's about people finding each other. But shortly after Seth and I find love, it's taken away from us by this terrible accident. *The Fly* is actually very sad."

Davis' Veronica Quaife—like most of the roles in Cronenbeg's remake—marginally resembles the original's counterpart, devoted wife Patricia Owens, though both women stick with their flies—uh, men—through the final swat. Davis says that she enjoyed the 1958 classic.

juice, their style, the attempt was to make them happen as much on the set as possible," Davis notes. "They wouldn't be that super *Star Wars* hi-tech, but would be more authentic and gloomy looking."

Fortunately for the dear departed Maitlands, death actually winds up strengthening their relationship. "A nice thing happens to us," observes Davis. "We mature. I think it was Tim who said that we become more human once we're dead. Once we're dead, we have to confront all these new outrageous experiences. And we help each other in a great way. We become involved with other people and helping them."

Burton, Davis explains, "had the clearest idea of what he wanted" of any director she has worked with. "When I first met Tim," she recalls, "he had drawn—he's a great illustrator—pictures of what he wanted the set to look like. And when we got on the set months later, it looked *exactly* like the pictures, like a 3-D photograph of his drawings. At every moment, he really knew what it should be and what it was all about. It was refreshing. If anybody had a sensibility about this, it was Tim Burton, and I just swallowed his whole idea for this thing."

Davis was also on screen with Goldblum in the science-fiction musical comedy *Earth Girls Are Easy*, directed by musical video veteran Julien (*Absolute Beginners*) Temple. "It's a very weird movie," says Davis. "I play this manicurist from the Valley, and aliens all covered in fur—Jeff and two other fellows [Jim Carrey, Damon Wayans]—land in my swimming pool. They have to stay for the weekend, so I try to help them out and I bring them into the salon where I work. Julie Brown is the hairstylist and she shaves them and waxes them. It turns out they're cute guys, so we end up going out with them. And I fall in love with Jeff's character.

"There's singing and some dancing. The aliens don't actually sing, but they come from a planet where they can make sounds. If you make a sound, they can copy it. So, they make up songs out of toilet flushings and any sounds we make here.

It's fun. It's an alien's view of the [San Fernando] Valley, how weird it is. Julien is British, so he actually *is* an alien. This is all his perception of the Valley, and he thinks it's pretty strange. It's not stupid, dumb or vulgar—it's naive and innocent."

Davis earned an Oscar for her supporting role in *The Accidental Tourist* and won acclaim for her turn in *Thelma and Louise*. She's now married to director Renny (*Die Hard II*) Harlin with whom she made *Cutthroat Island*. She wasn't a part of the sequel, *The Fly II*—in fact, her character (played by another actress) is in the movie only long enough to die. Nevertheless, Davis is developing her own film sequel *Flies*. It picks up the story on a different tack.

Pondering the possible follow-ups brings to mind the *original* ending of Cronenberg's *The Fly*, a climax which played with the idea of whether or not Veronica Quaife would keep the baby she conceived with mutated scientist Seth Brundle. "After the scene where I kill him, we see me in bed. I seem upset and I fall asleep and have this dream," Davis recalls. "I'm in this beautiful forest and I come along to this tree with this cocoon or something on it. It opens up and inside is this perfect little human baby. But then, it sprouts wings and flies away. It's all beautiful and magical.

"Then, it's back to my face and I'm smiling at this vision I'm having. And the camera pans down and we see that I'm nine months pregnant, that I've gone through with it. It's like, 'Oh my God, she's gonna do it!' I always liked that ending.

"Finally, they were worried that the effect might look funny instead of touching. Also, David Cronenberg decided—and I think he's right—that the ending that's there is so powerful that it shouldn't have been followed with something else."

For Davis, the ending worked because she never saw *The Fly* as just a SF movie or an effects film, it was always something special. What does she consider the theme of *The Fly*?

"What will you do for love?" Geena Davis says. "How far will you go?"

When the house you're haunting needs to be exorcised of humans, call the ghostest with the mostest, Beetlejuice (Michael Keaton).

VULCAN LEGEND

By Steve Swires, Randy & Jean-Marc Lofficier
and Marc Shapiro

Perhaps no audience in history has been as conspicuously enthusiastic as the remarkably enduring worldwide fan following for *Star Trek*. This intense level of public interest assures every *Trek* film and TV show of virtually microscopic examination. Such rigorous scrutiny might actually dissuade some nervous director from venturing into this potentially explosive critical minefield. But Leonard Nimoy, who made his long-awaited directorial debut with 1984's *Star Trek III: The Search for Spock*, emerged relatively unscathed.

"I was quite satisfied with the public reception," says Nimoy who, needless to say, portrays the half-human, half-Vulcan science-fiction hero named Spock. "The movie told the story I expected it to tell. The message I tried to get across was conveyed well. The audience responded to the characters as I hoped they would. And I was very pleased that the picture did so well financially."

Ever since he first pointed his ears and raised his eyebrows as Vulcan Science Officer Spock, Nimoy has firmly believed it would be best for *Star Trek* if *he* were in creative command. "Directing *Star Trek* has been in my mind since 1966," he notes. "Bill Shatner and I wanted to direct episodes of the TV series. We asked for that opportunity during the second and third seasons, but we met with resistance."

Interested in directing for years, Nimoy directed theater in the '50s and had a "steady sprinkling of directing experience" throughout his career (*Night Gallery*, *The Powers of Matthew Star*, *T. J. Hooker*).

And once firmly ensconsed as director, Nimoy felt he knew *Star Trek* far better than studio execs. "The only time there was any conflict about the movie's content happened during pre-production, when I said I was satisfied with the final script and was ready to start shooting. The executives had some reservations about ending the picture on Vulcan. I wanted to end the film by bringing Spock to Vulcan, and going through the ritual. I believed it *would* work.

"Not being so familiar with *Star Trek*, the executives didn't

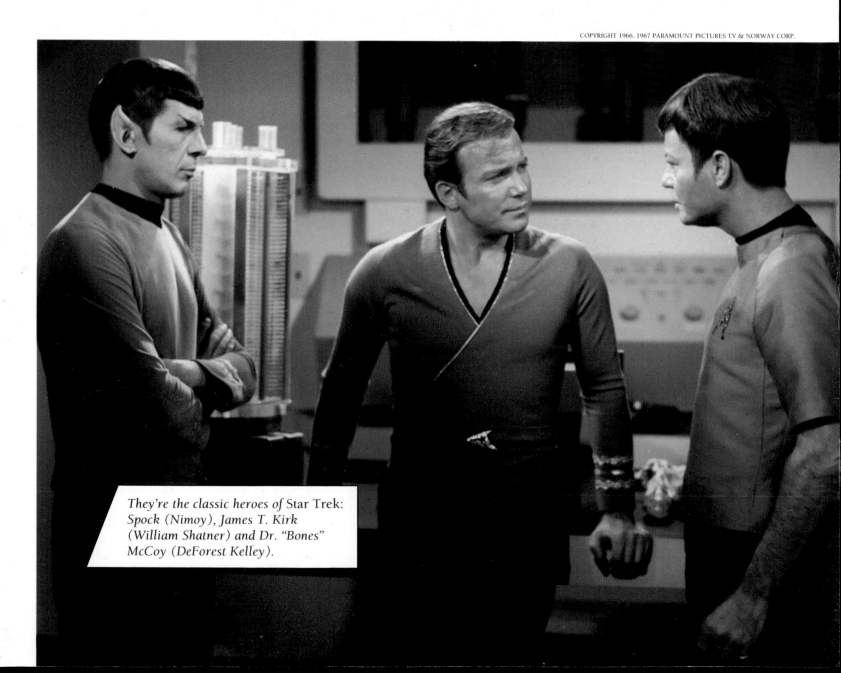

They're the classic heroes of Star Trek: *Spock (Nimoy), James T. Kirk (William Shatner) and Dr. "Bones" McCoy (DeForest Kelley).*

It has been a long *Trek* for Nimoy. And no one can be certain whether it's truly over yet.

the actors, the art director, the cinematographer, special FX people.

"Everything I know has been tapped—acting, drama, photography, production; my taste in color, composition, structure, editing. I was *thoroughly* gratified by the experience.

"*The Search for Spock* is a *major* statement on my part to *Star Trek* fans. Whatever they may have heard or thought in the past, *here* is how I feel about these characters. I hope my *love* for *Star Trek* is on the screen."

Most people were pleased with his maiden directorial effort. However, Nimoy *was* criticized by some angry fans, who were infuriated by two unexpected plot twists—what they perceived as the gratuitous death of Kirk's illegitimate son, David Marcus, and the cavalier destruction of the beloved starship *Enterprise*. "Their reaction was understandable," Nimoy acknowledges. "The fans *should* react personally. We didn't make those decisions lightly, or in a vacuum. I understand these plot developments take place in a very real environment, which is *Star Trek* and its audience. I'm aware of that reality."

understand what that sequence would mean to the audience. They tried to convince me to substitute a different ending. They wanted to end with the dramatic escape from the Genesis planet, getting Kirk and Spock on board the Klingon *Bird of Prey*, reviving Spock in the sick bay, doing a little tag scene and going home.

"I argued *vehemently* that we had to have the sequence on Vulcan. Showing Spock on his planet, among his people, trying to remember his friends, would be a moving scene. I managed to convince them that I wanted to do it *my* way, and they agreed. I didn't discuss the film with them again until I showed them my first cut."

Having waited so long to call his own shots, Nimoy has learned the value of patience. "Directing *The Search for Spock* was the most completely challenging opportunity I've *ever* had," he observes. "It called on every resource I've developed during the last 30 years in this business—working with

Nimoy believes both these troubling events were properly motivated by legitimate artistic considerations. "The death of David Marcus has its roots in all of the classic tragic forms," he explains. "It is the vengeance of fate wreaked upon the flawed person who created the problem. David is the character who must pay the price for whatever wrongs he has done, and for whatever pain and suffering he has inflicted—intentionally or not—on others. He put the Genesis device into operation prematurely.

"My major concern regarding David's death was the accuracy of the scientific aspect. I thought we had better tread carefully there, because, in effect, we were saying that scientists can't always be depended upon to be—you should pardon the expression—*logical*. We were accusing a scientist of prematurely finishing an experiment with which he had become impatient. I checked with some very important scientists on this subject, and they told me it happens all the time."

Equally justifiable, in Nimoy's judgment, was the elimination of the *Enterprise*. "Frankly, I thought it was well executed," he maintains. "We didn't destroy the *Enterprise* for cheap or inflammatory reasons but because therein lay drama. It was a certain kind of drama which you can do in motion pictures, but you can't do on television.

"As [director] Nicholas Meyer said about killing Spock in *Star Trek II*, 'We're not playing games here. This isn't a red herring, like they do on TV. Spock is *really dead*.' Destroying the *Enterprise* was the same. It was a valid dramatic choice, not a transparent TV ploy.

"For me, the film really deals with the responsibilities of friendship. The crew members are confronted with a personal decision that each must make. They set out on a personal mission, because of a hope they have. There's also a sense of *The Seven Samurai*—a gathering of the group who will try to do the honorable thing."

Constrained by the storyline, Nimoy was necessarily limited in the amount of attention he could devote to each cast member. "We carry a lot of baggage with us when we arrive to make a *Star Trek* movie," he points out. "We have a large group of characters, and it's difficult to adequately spotlight all of them. Each time we add a new character, we take away screen time from the others. The question is, can we properly service the story and the key characters and also satisfy all the fans who want to see their favorite person?

"I come from an actor's roots, so I knew that the actors wanted to contribute to the film," he emphasizes. "I have great respect for *all* the *Star Trek* cast and the characters they play. I have a strong sense of what they bring to those characters and what the audience has always loved about them. Each character has its own moments. They're treated like *real* people, rather than just button-pushers in the background."

As for *Star Trek IV: The Voyage Home*, which Nimoy also directed, "It was the most fun I've had playing Spock in a long time. When we left Spock in *Star Trek III*, he was disoriented, trying to figure out who's who, until he finally managed to recognize Jim Kirk. So, it's quite a different Spock than that seen before—he's funny and charming."

By "wiping the slate clean" after *Star Trek III*, Nimoy gave himself the chance to try things with Spock's character that he couldn't do before. "We see him going through a growing up process," Nimoy explains. "Spock looks kind of bemused and is wondering about what's happening—'What am I supposed to do about this?' His memory is back: facts, figures, data, history and so on. But, on the other hand, his sensitivities and sensibilities, his awareness of social attitudes and conduct and how to function in society are still a little bit askew—that made it a lot of fun."

The director very definitely didn't want to do the same film he had done before. "I made a conscious decision *not* to repeat myself," he announces. "I wanted *Trek IV* to be an adventure that's fun to watch. After life, death and resurrection, we must turn to a *lighter* approach. That doesn't mean silly comedy, just good *Star Trek* with a more humorous angle. We did it often on

Exploring The Final Frontier, *Spock encountered a brother, Sybok (Laurence Luckinbill), with his own agenda.*

Venturing into The Undiscovered Country, *Spock learned a painful truth from his protege Valeris (Kim Cattrall).*

the TV series in 'A Piece of the Action,' 'The Trouble with Tribbles' and the Harry Mudd stories. In a sense, it's the completion of a trilogy. It wasn't intentional, but it has worked out that way. *Star Trek II, III* and *IV* form a set."

Star Trek IV's story, of course, centers on a fateful journey through time that the *Enterprise* crew must undertake. Their mission: to bring back a pair of humpback whales—a species extinct in the team's own future epoch. "We had agreed—the studio, myself and writer/producer Harve Bennett—that the concept would essentially be a time travel story. I did some research which had to do with contemporary scientific concerns about the future. And, of course, one of the big, big scientific concerns is endangered species and loss of species.

"There are what Harvard biologist named Edward O. Wilson refers to as 'keystone' species. The keystone theory means that, if you build a house of cards, you can take this card out or that card out and the house won't fall down, but at a certain point, you get down to the *keystone* cards which really hold up our planet's ecological structure. We may not even be sure which are the keystone species. But you pull one out and the whole thing starts to crumble.

"So, I became intrigued with the idea that we have a problem erupting in the 23rd century that can only be resolved by using an element from an extinct species, one that was allowed to die or was killed off. The future scientists are at a loss because they cannot synthetically replace this natural thing. Finally, it came down to whales."

Shooting on location in San Francisco was, according to Nimoy, one of the highlights of *Trek IV*. It's not often, after all, that the *Enterprise* crew gets the chance to mingle with real people on the street. "It was great," says Nimoy. "People like us. They know who we are, and they like the *Star Trek* movies. I loved being there. I loved the whole idea of bringing *Star Trek* home to today."

As once again both actor and director, Nimoy was quite busy on *Star Trek IV*. "Acting in and directing the same project are sometimes frustrating," he confesses. "Particularly when you have to be in a scene, and you know that there are things going on behind you that you cannot see. You would like to be able to have an eye in the back of your head. I had

the support of a very good camera department, and Bill Shatner was helpful in that, when he wasn't in a shot, he was watching. Also, there were the other actors, all of whom I trust. They got me past the tough times."

Shatner, of course, was in charge of the next film in the saga, directing *Star Trek V: The Final Frontier*. It gave Nimoy new challenges. "There has been what I consider an interesting kind of arc to Spock in these films. He died in *Star Trek II* and is brought back to life in *III* but with not a whole lot of his grey matter operating. By the end of *Star Trek IV*, we find that he has sucked up a lot of information and is standing on his feet again. Now in *Trek V*, he's given the presence of his brother, which tests his loyalty. These kinds of changes are the things that continue to make Spock an interesting character to play."

Nimoy, fresh from directing *Three Men and a Baby* and then *The Good Mother*, laughingly offers that it wasn't difficult to come on to the *Star Trek V* set and just act.

"Believe me, just acting was a *wonderful* break for me," he smiles. "I had just finished four films in a row with almost no break in between and I really enjoyed the idea that Bill would be carrying the load and that I could sit in my trailer and take it easy."

But not that easy, as Nimoy discloses in his assessment of Shatner as a director. "Bill's such a physical guy to begin with and I immediately found that was going to spill over into this film. There was much more running and jumping that I normally like to do. I was constantly going up the elevator, down the stairs, across the cliff, down the rocks. We shot in the heat of the day and the cold of the night. *Star Trek V* was a fun film to do, but it was also a very difficult one."

The movie's early campfire sequences with Kirk, Spock and McCoy, a calm counter to the action-oriented nature of the rest of the film, hold some pleasant memories.

"I felt the idea of having Kirk, Spock and McCoy [DeForest Kelley] sitting down and being with each other with no adventure involved and nothing to deal with was wonderful. It put the whole *Star Trek* experience on a very human scale and, in a very positive way, recognized the validity of the relationship these three have had over the years."

The introduction of Laurence Luckinbill as Spock's half-brother Sybok proved a further test of Spock's emotional mettle. "Larry and I understood from the beginning what the nature of the relationship should be and what the scenes between us called for. But there were some instinctive moments in those scenes that weren't in the script and that ended up being used. There was the moment where Larry unexpectedly grabbed me in that bearhug and I withdrew. Bill saw it, liked it and we ended up using it in that scene."

Although *Trek V* was somewhat of a box-office disappointment, Kirk, Spock, McCoy and company were soon called back for yet another film, *Star Trek VI: The Undiscovered Country*. In May 1990, Nimoy lunched with then-Paramount president Frank Mancuso.

"Frank told me that he would like to have one more *Star Trek* with the old crew to commemorate the 25th anniversary [in 1991] and have the whole thing go out in style. I went away from that meeting, thought about it and came up with a story idea that would parallel current world events and at the same time would give some sense of the *Enterprise* crew having completed the essential mission.

"I told Frank the story and suggested that we get Nick Meyer to write and direct it. I met with Nick, spent an entire day telling him my idea and why I thought it would work as a fitting final film. He responded very well and immediately began to build on my story."

Meyer completed the script with co-writer Denny Martin Flinn, and it was subsequently circulated to the *Trek* cast by the studio. Nimoy recalls their reactions.

"They understood the story and it was clear that everybody would have their moments in the movie. It was a very emotional time for everybody. We were getting together for our last reunion. We knew we were never going to do this again."

At least all of them weren't going to do it again. Kirk, Scotty and Chekov did, of course, return for the first *Next Generation* film, 1994's *Star Trek Generations*.

Nimoy had already made his move into *The Next Generation*, appearing in the two-part adventure "Unification." "Things happen when they're supposed to," he notes. "You let things unfold as they should. It seemed like the right time and all the right reasons to do it.

"Returning to television was comfortable for me. I know the character so well, even though I was working with a different cast. But, Spock is Spock, and bringing this character back to TV was coming full circle for me.

"I played Spock differently," he continues, "but only in the sense that it was a different story and he was 75 years older. Things had definitely changed for Spock in *The Next Generation* universe."

Nimoy is reminded of a 1986 comment in which, in regard to *Star Trek: The Next Generation*'s premiere, he wondered if Gene Roddenberry could once again "catch lightning in a bottle." Nimoy now believes that Roddenberry and company actually acccomplished that task.

"*The Next Generation* was a well-done, logical extension of the premise that the original *Star Trek* laid down. The characters and the stories were consistently good, and it lasted longer than our show did, which has to tell you something."

Now an accomplished director, Nimoy has many avenues open to him. Looking back on the six *Star Trek* motion pictures, he's notably candid.

"I wasn't at all pleased with *Star Trek: The Motion Picture*. I felt let down by the whole experience. We all got up for it, but we just didn't get it off. There was no personal satisfaction in making that picture.

"Then, I was very pleased and impressed with *Star Trek II*. It was a moving experience for me in that it was the end of Spock, and it was a well-made movie that got *Star Trek* back on the right track. *Star Trek III* was a wonderful, joyous discovery for me. It was a rebirth in that Spock was coming back to life and I was beginning my life as a director.

"*Star Trek IV* was a great ride in which the story, the ideas, the fun and all the production elements just fell into place. For me, the highlight of *Star Trek V* was the joy of watching Bill [Shatner] direct. And now, *Star Trek VI* was the end [for the original cast].

"I thought we were finished several times," Leonard Nimoy confesses. "I felt we were finished at the [original TV series'] second season's end, but then, there was that big outcry and we were renewed for a third season. After the third season, I thought, 'Now we're really done.' In '79, we made the first movie and I thought, 'OK, now we've made the movie and now we're done.' None of us could have predicted that we *might* never be done with *Star Trek*."

BELOVED STARMAN

By Brian Lowry and Christine Menefee

An alien assuming human form can be anyone. And indeed, in the 1984 film, *Starman*, the alien showed up looking just like Jeff Bridges. When it came time for a TV version, it was up to Robert Hays—best known as the nervous pilot of the *Airplane!* films—to get serious and become Starman.

That doesn't mean Hays has lost his sense of humor. Take the sphere, for example, the handy-dandy silver orb that Starman calls upon to get himself out of particularly difficult predicaments. The TV series' producers, the actor reports impishly, requested that he " 'Be sure to use the word "sphere," because we don't want to get into the habit of calling them, you know'—and I said, 'What, *balls*?' "So, of course, I have to call them that and tell people I'm clutching my balls. I'm a rotten kid."

Indeed, if straight answers and Hays are at all acquainted, they're certainly not the best of friends. Even between scenes, he's constantly firing off one-liners—for his own amusement as much as anything else. "It's a good idea to keep a fun atmosphere on the set," he says.

Still, for all his clowning, Hays is happy to be Starman—to have the opportunity to do what he believes is a quality show.

The other reason he opted for the role, he says, involves the creative talents behind the scenes, including Michael Douglas (who produced the film), producers Mike Gray and John Mason (they scripted *The China Syndrome*), and executive producers Jim Hirsch and Jim Henerson.

"I thought, 'If I'm going to do a TV series, I would like to be with a quality

bunch, good folks.' I'm stuck with these people and they're stuck with me, so it's nice if you all like each other," he notes.

Hays does get a bit peeved at those who compare his work to Bridges' Oscar-nominated portrayal. The fact that Starman returns and inhabits a different body, much like a suit of clothes, is another reason Hays took the role.

That accounts for the difference in appearance, since Starman now resembles a deceased photojournalist named Paul Forrester, traveling the country with his son Scott (Barnes) in search of the boy's mother, Jenny Hayden (Erin Gray).

"I hadn't seen the movie until I decided I was going to do the series, and then I saw it on cable," Hays admits. "I thought about *not* doing it because of the movie. The new body was one of the main reasons for being able to do the series. I've been asked, 'How do you like playing Jeff Bridges?' And I said I'm not."

Hays and the producers made a conscious decision not to emulate Bridges' characterization of herky-jerky motions and stilted speech; rather, the humor stems from Starman's naiveté and tendency to take Earth colloquialisms literally.

When someone tells him he's "wet behind the ears," for example, the character checks, and is puzzled by his dry lobes.

While expressing admiration for Bridges' approach, Hays

COPYRIGHT 1986, 1987 COLUMBIA PICTURES TELEVISION

That's the silver sphere in Starman's hands, though Hays naughtily calls it by another, funnier name.

believes trying to reproduce it on a TV series wouldn't have worked for a number of reasons. "He already did that," Hays contends. "Starman was smoothing out by the film's end.

"Now, he has had all the time to assimilate human behavior, knowing he has to fit in much better than before. He's a fairly intelligent being, so he could figure that out rather quickly."

To retain the character's bird-like movements, Hays suggests, would have eventually driven both the star and the audience nuts. "This is something we're going to do every single week. We're not doing Shakespeare here, babe. We're not doing *Richard III*, or some characterization that requires you to go into heavy character work week after week, month after month. You've got to do something that's comfortable, that you can handle, that doesn't drive you crazy."

Although the character is an alien, Hays says he and Starman do have one thing in common: "He has a childlike innocence. I'm childlike anyway, so I don't have to worry about that," he says. "I just have to take my jaded side and make that innocent.

"Starman has been a little bit dumb here and there, and he's becoming smarter. He's learning how to act, learning what the word 'devious' means and how to use it against Earth people."

Although the series was cancelled after only one year, *Starman* established quite a loyal following led by the fans of the Spotlight Starman movement. Hays remarks that "the Spotlight *Starman* folk—a group of people so intelligent and dedicated, are doing wonderful things, and I appreciate it. This is, to me, the highest compliment I've *ever* had. It isn't often an actor gets jobs that make him feel that good."

Revealing that those involved in the series still keep in touch, Hays says that he and "C.B. [Christopher Daniel Barnes], Michael [Cavanaugh], and of course Patrick [Culliton]—he's one of my closest friends—sometimes talk about *Starman* and the way we feel about the show."

In the early stages of planning for *Starman*, the series' creative personnel discussed its possibilities. "When Mike Gray, Jim Hirsch, John Mason and the others and I first started talking

about *Starman*, the most appealing aspect of the show was the fact that while it's to a great degree about humanity, this guy [the alien played by Hays] is the being with the most humanity in the whole show. He has a completely open mind. He's not American, Russian or Nicaraguan. He's holding up a mirror to people. Of course, there will always be some people whose mirror is," Hays pauses, looking for the right metaphor, "a piece of wood."

However, Hays "didn't realize" the TV series would have such a strong impact. But then, the actor muses, "I'm always surprised when people like the things I do. I wouldn't be surprised if *Starman* is ranked as one of the most special TV shows of all time."

Fans would be quick to agree, but Hays says he's talking about the fans themselves. "This is one of the special effects of the show that everybody is noticing. The campaign [to revive the series] is *not* just about *Starman*. It's about our concept of television and what we would like it to be. By keeping this alive, the fans are making a real strong statement to the network and to the whole community. If we learn one thing from this experience, it's to speak up *before* a show is cancelled."

What does Hays think of people who are willing to see *Starman* return on *any* terms, even inferior ones? "Some people are just leaping on the bandwagon, and others are more level-headed. To me, it's more important to get a *good* show on the air,

Says Hays, "We had such a real special time making Starman. *The fans are keeping it alive."*

Hays enjoyed making the Airplane! *films, but he cautions, "I didn't want to be doing them for the rest of my days."*

even if it's a *different* show. Of course, there could never be another *Starman*," he notes. "What I want is to get the best thing happening that I can. "The problem is, finding good shows, good scripts, good things. But that's what I'm trying to do."

Before becoming a science-fiction hero in *Starman*, Hays conquered his fear of flying as Ted Stryker in *Airplane!* "No one knew *Airplane!* was going to be a hit," he concedes. "No one ever does."

Hays took up acting in college, then spent some time living in his Volkswagen bus ("Interviewers really seem to enjoy that," he points out) as an actual starving actor.

After the *Airplane!* films, Hays has flown quietly through a variety of TV and theatrical projects. On the genre front, he co-starred in "The Ledge" segment of *Cat's Eye*, pairing him with character actor Kenneth (*Dune*) McMillan. Hays spent much of the time standing on a ledge, about 25 feet off the ground. "They had a big long shot, from way back, so they had no cushions or anything to break the fall," he recalls. "Ken

McMillan was such a good actor. He taught, so it was like being in acting class."

But it's *Starman* that continues to hold a special place in this actor's heart. "Doing the series was tough, but it was wonderful. We all had such a real special time, we had a *great* time."

And the series, in reruns on the Sci-Fi Channel, continues to garner new fans. How does Hays feel about all these new fans? He says the family-like spirit on the *Starman* set "seems to have gone on to the fans, and the fans are keeping it alive. The fans are now one more extension of the family."

One Christmas, his fan club sent Hays a six-foot stocking embroidered with the titles of his many projects containing a great many "absolutely *wonderful* things from *Starman* people—Star People—all around the country. It was remarkable. I sure did appreciate that."

One gift in particular seems to have touched Robert Hays. "Did you know," he asks, "they named a star—you know, up there—after *me*? My gosh."

KLINGON WARRIOR

By David McDonnell and Ian Spelling

The Romulan lay dying and of all the hundreds aboard the *U.S.S. Enterprise*, only the Klingon warrior Worf could save him. Only the Klingon possessed the compatible ribosomes, the correct blood type, for the life-saving transfusion. Yet, it was the Romulans who, years ago, murdered Worf's parents.

"*This* Romulan did not murder your parents," the doctor tells him. The second-in-command advises him. And the Captain begs him.

But, ultimately, it must be Worf's decision alone. He lets the Romulan die.

"I was concerned about that," admits Michael Dorn, who played Worf on *Star Trek: The Next Generation*. "I thought that

was a real risk on the producers' part to let that happen. I called the producers up and said, 'Explain this to me. Before I do it, explain *why* you want to go this way. I have a little trepidation about it.'

"We've gotten used to Worf being almost human. You look at characters for years, no matter how alien, and suddenly, they *become* human. You expect them to act like humans, since they're around humans. As human beings, we always put human qualities to everything—dogs, cats, aliens. And they said, 'Worf is not a human. He's an alien.' In that episode, 'The Enemy,' the producers wanted to show that Worf is *not* subject to human morality because he's not human. He's a Klingon. I couldn't argue with that. Then, I got into the acting and wondered how can I do this, what am I going to dredge up to make it work, so that the audience believes Worf is right in letting the Romulan die. It became a challenge."

For Dorn, it also became a highlight of the series' third season. "The shows that really do Worf justice aren't the ones that are particularly about him," the actor observes. "But 'The Enemy' was a wonderful show because I had three scenes, one with Gates McFadden, one with Jonathan Frakes, and one with Patrick Stewart. And each of them wanted Worf to do it, to save the Romulan. Dr. Crusher says, 'What's the matter with you, where's your humanity?' Riker says, 'Hey, I'm not going to tell you what to do. I'm going to tell you what I think, but I'm *not* going to tell you what to do. You're on your own, buddy.'

"And the Captain says—he's very manipulative, and that's what Patrick told me he liked about the scene—'The Romulan ship will be here pretty soon, won't it?' 'Yes.' 'Just think about it. A Romulan dying at the hands of the Federation.' 'I have thought about that, too, sir.' 'So, the Romulan's better off to us alive than dead?' 'Yes, Captain.' 'Well, Worf, it's very difficult being a captain.' I don't have a bunch of dialogue. 'Worf, you wouldn't complain even if you had cause, you're such a brilliant soldier.' He's just buttering me up."

From the beginning of his tour of duty on board the *Enterprise*, Dorn realized his character would not be prominent in every episode. "I didn't care," he says. "I said, fine, whenever he does something, I'll just try to make it memorable. If they give me two lines, I'll make them a *great* two lines. It's not anything spectacular. It's what actors do—all the good actors I would hope to be like: Jack Nicholson, Robert De Niro, Sidney Poitier. I also admire Patrick Stewart because he can move you. That's what's important.

"In Tasha Yar's funeral scene ['Skin of Evil'], everybody played their parts wonderfully. And they showed Patrick on camera and you *didn't know* what he was going to do. Is he going to cry? That's the edge. That's what got me. Only very seldom have I seen this work. I would have to have Patrick's ability because he *does* move people.

"With 'The Enemy' it was very easy for me to do that scene where he asked me to give blood because he was right there. The director—a great director, David Carson—told me, 'This is

"Worf should never become a nice guy," vows Michael Dorn, who plays this science-fiction hero.

Worf got a promotion—and all wet—in Star Trek Generations. *He looks forward to further Trek films.*

Several seventh season episodes hinted at future romance between Worf and Deanna Troi (Marina Sirtis).

it. Picard's going to *order* you to give blood and that's going to be the end of it. It's off your shoulders, you don't have to make the decision anymore, so you're happy.' I walk in there. 'Yes, sir. I understand, sir. I've thought about it.' And then he begs me. I want to do it, but he can't ask me to do it, he would have to *order* me to do it. It's just wonderful working with Patrick."

Playing this science-fiction hero is always a challenge. And Dorn has vowed that "Worf should never become a nice guy, a teddy bear."

If Worf were to evolve into a nicer guy, "he would lose his edge. He would become human and ineffective as a character because he's not dangerous any more. He doesn't mean it. He's a nice guy," explains Dorn, occasionally lapsing into the use of the personal pronoun "I" when he's actually referring to his Klingon alter-ego. "Everybody was sitting there watching 'The Enemy' and saying, 'He's *not* not going to do it. He'll give the blood. Worf, he's a great guy.' Suddenly, the Romulan's dead. Worf just went along about his business. The show ended. A couple of my friends thought that Worf was going to save the Romulan's life; they *knew* that I was going to save his life because I'm a nice guy. Wrong.

"I'm *not* a nice guy," Dorn says. "And that's what I liked about the whole thing."

As *The Next Generation* continued, Worf, while not a nice guy, became a bit more mellow. "At the series' beginning, Worf hated everybody," Dorn confesses. "He didn't like a child, Wesley, or a machine, Data, being on the Bridge. Worf had to respect Riker because he was a superior officer and Picard because he was a legend. Tasha Yar was the only one that Worf really liked or felt strongly about. She kicked butt as fast as he did.

"But in those early episodes, Worf felt that he was a better soldier than all of these people. That's the feeling I brought across. Now, his emotions have mellowed. Now, he tolerates them. And some very interesting things have happened."

Since the beginning of *The Next Generation*, Dorn has made Worf a Klingon like no other. He has seen the Klingons of the original series and the films, but to this day Dorn continues to take Gene Roddenberry's mandate at his word: "Forget all you've seen and heard, and make Worf your own character."

"They were all a certain way in the past. We've created a new type of Klingon. We've seen that they're not out of control. These are calculated, passionate people," he says. "They don't just grunt, growl and go around killing people for no apparent reason. I feel proud of that.

"I didn't set out, I must say, to go, 'Hey, I want to be the model for all Klingons.' I just wanted to do the best I could to make the character very interesting and make him stand out from anything we've seen. And I decided to make Worf a character who's treading the edge."

Dorn appreciates that *The Next Generation*'s writing staff has gone to such great lengths to explore various aspects of Worf's life. Still, as an actor, he would like more. "What they'll do with other characters on our show is have a situation, and then they'll explain *why* the person feels a certain way or why

the character acted in a particular fashion. What they've done with Worf is put him in a situation where he does something and the show ends. There's usually no explanation of why he has done what he has done. Most of the time it's like 'Reunion.'

"After I kill Duras," Dorn explains, "Picard says, 'You're on the ship. You've got to keep in line. If you can't, you've got to leave. Can you do it?' I say, 'Yes, sir.' and that was the end of it. He didn't ask why Worf killed this guy or say it was the wrong thing to do. If he had, then I could say, 'I acted in the Klingon tradition.' I guess they're trying not to give away all there is to Worf. Once they give it all away, Worf would get boring. If you can predict the way he's going to react and know everything about him, then there's *nothing* left to write.

"But that's just a general overview. Specifically, I loved 'Reunion.' Many things I talked about with the writers *were* in there. I liked 'The Drumhead' too. Jean Simmons! This is a star. It was wonderful to work with her. It was a very good episode. Of course, Jonathan directed it, and I'm a very big Jonathan Frakes fan. The end of the show was a nice scene. Once again, it was Worf and Picard. Worf's going, 'I can't believe I did this,' and Picard says, 'Hey, this is the way things are. It's unbelievable, it's terrible, but vigilance.' It's such a powerful scene. That, I think, is what *Star Trek* is all about."

Other series highlights included working with Suzie Plakson, who portrayed K'Ehleyr, Worf's one-time mate and the mother of their child, Alexander (Brian Bonsall). Despite the character's popularity with Dorn and fans, K'Ehleyr perished in "Reunion." "She turned into a wonderful character. It's too bad she got killed. The fans really loved her. Unknowingly," Dorn reveals, "I contributed to her death. I was talking to the writer. He asked what would set Worf off. I said that it would have to be something that would just piss him off no end. We talked about his honor. I said, 'He has already lost that,' so we threw out ideas. I thought her death was a good idea at the time. I always hate to see characters get killed, especially good characters, but it seemed the only thing that would piss Worf off to where he would forget about Starfleet, forget about rules and regulations, and kill this guy who murdered K'Ehleyr."

Dorn, of course, was the first to make the jump to the big screen with *Star Trek VI: The Undiscovered Country*, in which he portrays Lt. Worf's grandfather. He's Colonel Worf, a Klingon lawyer who must defend Kirk and McCoy when they're put on trial for the assassination of the Klingon Chancellor.

"I didn't want to play Colonel Worf too differently from Lt. Worf," he says. "It's hard to play a character, in terms of trying to keep him Klingon. Though he's all the things a Klingon is, Worf is also eloquent, introspective, sensitive and deep, all in a very nasty way. That's what I tried to bring to Colonel Worf.

"We are all part of our parents. I'm like my father, and he was like my grandfather. I tried to show there is something of Lt. Worf in Colonel Worf. I was trying to show where Worf of *The Next Generation* got his passion."

Now, of course, the entire *Next Generation* crew has launched into theaters with *Star Trek Generations*. "Personally, to do a movie every two or three years is wonderful, because we

would be open to do other things," Dorn says. "On a series, that's all you can do, all you usually have time to do. *Next Generation* films are a blessing."

Trek fandom seems to greatly appreciate Dorn's efforts at creating a believable, noble, *alien* warrior. Worf's popularity has spawned an increasing number of Klingon fan clubs, something that in pre-*Next Generation* days might have been blasphemy. "I feel good thinking I had a hand in it. There has always been a Klingon faction in *Trek*dom, but since our show and the later films, they've become more prominent. It's especially a result of our show, because there's a Klingon on the Bridge."

In fact, Michael Dorn quite likes his place in *Star Trek*. He knows that once you're in it, you're in it forever, a part of an ongoing phenomenon. "It's a strange sort of existence. Suddenly, you're thrust into this limelight of conventions, fans, expectations and a history," he understates. "There's a 30-year bloodline of characters and stories. We've meant a lot to many people."

MAJOR PLAYER

By Ian Spelling

The reaction to Kira and to *Deep Space Nine* has been quite amazing," says Nana Visitor, "and I *never* take it for granted. I read all of the mail that comes to me. Every single letter means so much to me."

Visitor lucked into her *Trek* experience as a science-fiction heroine. Actress Michelle Forbes, who played the recurring *Next Generation* character Ensign Ro, turned down an offer from *DS9* executive producers/creators Rick Berman and Michael Piller to transfer her Bajoran character to the new series. That left a Bajoran void to be filled by Visitor, who was hired to portray Major Kira Nerys, a former Bajoran freedom fighter serving aboard *DS9* as First Officer to Commander Benjamin Sisko (Avery Brooks.)

The actress is pleased because her good fortune didn't come at Forbes' expense. "Michelle made a life decision in not taking the role," says the actress, "so I was able to make a life decision in taking it. Hopefully, she's as happy about her decision as I am with mine."

Kira has become one of *DS9*'s most popular characters.

Fans appreciate her brains; brawn, spunk and sensitivity. Constable Odo (Rene Auberjonois) and Kira have developed a strong friendship, with echoes (on Odo's part) of unrequited love. Kira also appears to believe in Sisko and what he stands for as much as he does in her. The Major's relationships with the other senior officers aren't quite as well-defined, though Visitor gamely offers her thoughts on where they stand. "She has a friendship with Dax [Terry Farrell]—the kind you have with someone you have nothing in common with," she says. "Yet, Kira and Dax find a humor and a sameness in their differences. Doctor Bashir [Siddig El Fadil] can still annoy Kira. He's like the rich kid, the Beverly Hills kid on the block.

"Bashir has all the training, all the advantages. Though Kira believes they're hard-won, she can still be very short with him. She had to fight for everything every inch of the way, and that creates conflict. I think there's a deep respect and camaraderie between Chief O'Brien [Colm Meaney] and Kira, but that's a relationship we need to explore more.

"Quark [Armin Shimerman] is an interesting subject," continues Visitor. "There has been true dislike, true disdain, and yet there's a certain understanding. I have to say there's an affection Kira has for Quark. It's almost as if she'll continue to hate what Ferengis are, but if Quark were in true danger, her instinct would be to come to his aid."

From the very beginning, Kira has figured prominently in the series' action and captured the imagination of fans, who have enjoyed watching the character's struggle to balance her cause (Bajor) and her new responsibilities (the Federation). Many of the episodes that prominently feature Kira bring back very specific memories for Visitor.

" 'Emissary' [the pilot] was like making a film," she says. "We were given a lot of control in creating our characters and a lot of respect. Some shows want you to deliver what you're supposed to deliver and then shut up. David Carson, our director, would let us do what we *needed* to build the characters. I ended up stalking around a lot in that show. I felt like Kira was a trapped cat in much of it. The experience was great. It was my first inkling that *Deep Space Nine* wouldn't try to limit me, but would push me as an actress."

"Battle Lines" still has many *Trek* fans talking — especially about its violent action. Kira, Sisko, Bashir and Kai Opaka (Camille Saviola) crash-landed on Ennis, where two warring factions fought the same war forever. The only hope for Ennis was the Kai, who died in the crash and, like the fighting Ennis, returned to life. The episode forced Kira to watch her spiritual leader die, be resur-

Kira likes Quark (Armin Shimerman)—sort of. "If he were in true danger," Visitor says, "her instinct would be to come to his aid."

DANNY FELD

At the edge of the final frontier, the crew of Space Station Deep Space Nine confront alien dangers every day.

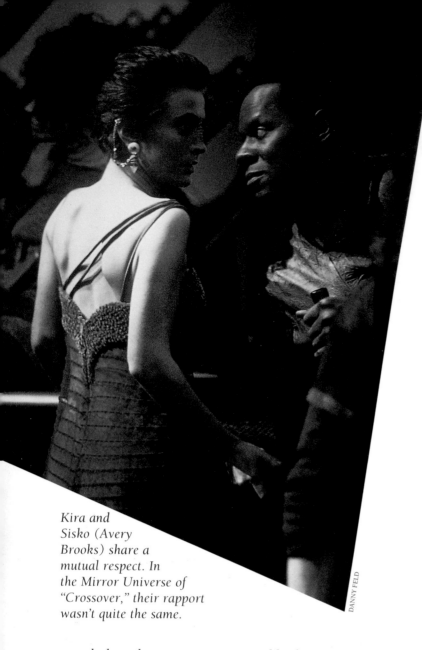

Kira and Sisko (Avery Brooks) share a mutual respect. In the Mirror Universe of "Crossover," their rapport wasn't quite the same.

DANNY FELD

rected, then choose to stay to try and broker peace.

"It was very interesting in that I got to push the envelope. People are always uncomfortable seeing people's emotions," Visitor says. "In the scene where the Kai dies, I could have faked the emotions completely and no one would have known because of how it was shot. The truth is it was an honest breakdown of someone believing their mentor and matriarchal figure was gone from their life forever.

"That rawness of emotions Kira displayed made many people uncomfortable. It was uncomfortable for *me* to watch. Yet, there's something I delight in about displaying those emotions. Taking my clothes off for a scene, to me, *isn't* challenging. What *is* challenging, and what I don't mind using to make people feel uncomfortable, is displaying raw emotion. Reaction to the episode was mixed. People wrote in to say it made them really uncomfortable or that it affected them greatly. Either way is fine. It meant I had done my job."

"Progress" gave Visitor the opportunity to work with veteran actor Brian Keith, who played Mullibok, an old Bajoran farmer who refuses to leave the Bajoran moon, Jeraddo, when the Federation and Bajoran government seek to evacuate its inhabitants. "That was a delight," she says. "Working with Brian was stimulating. He pushed me to do more and more. It was also about finding Kira not on the offensive, really for the first time. It was Kira at rest."

"Dramatis Personae" more or less reflected a different side

of Kira, as an alien matrix altered the personalities of the space station's senior crew. The situation left a feisty, threatening Kira pitted against Sisko in a nasty struggle for control of *DS9*. "It was another facet of Kira we hadn't seen yet," explains the actress. "If there's one thing Kira usually doesn't do, it's manipulate people. She says what she means and that's it. To be manipulative and use her sexuality, another thing under most circumstances Kira wouldn't dream of, was fun to do."

The very next episode, "Duet," was a "bottle" episode—one with few cast members, effects or new sets, intended to keep the budget down. It turned into one of *Deep Space Nine*'s finest, most memorable hours. In it, Harris Yulin played Marritza, a Cardassian who may or may not be a hated war criminal responsible for the death of countless Bajorans. By the episode's end, when Marritza reveals his deep-seated sense of guilt, Kira can't help but feel sympathy and respect for a member of a people she desperately wants to loathe.

"It was a painful show to film," says Visitor. "The original script was *very* graphic. I remember reading paragraphs that made me cry. They were so graphic and horrifying, I took it all very seriously. Eventually, that material was all taken out. The atrocities were better off suggested than described in detail. Harris and I were able to communicate the horrors the Cardassians committed against the Bajorans without it being so spelled out."

Season one concluded with "In the Hands of the Prophets," in which the appearance of Bajoran spiritual leader Vedek Winn (Louise Fletcher) threatens to undo the tenuous alliance between Bajor and the Federation. The episode also set up the series' continuing conflict between Vedek Winn and Vedek Bareil (Philip Anglim), both of whom are vying to be named the next Kai. Bareil would become Kira's lover, only to later die tragically in "Life Support," while Winn would be selected Kai.

"It was so strange for me to see so many Bajorans at one time," says Visitor. "I also got to see the holy people in the Bajoran religious hierarchy. Working with Philip Anglim and Louise Fletcher was very exciting. It meant something that those people wanted to be on our show. It was also a personal triumph for me because doing that show meant we had done a whole season. Avery and I filmed the last scene on April 7, I sat down in Ops, in my uniform, with my nose and my earring, thinking where I was a year ago that day. Do you know what I was doing? I was giving birth to my son Buster on that *same* day."

Kira featured prominently in the second season's opening three-episode arc. In the first show, "The Homecoming," Kira and O'Brien rescued the Bajoran hero Li Nalas (Richard Beymer) from a Cardassian prison colony. The Bajoran terrorists of the Circle incited trouble in their efforts to create a Bajor for Bajorans only. By the episode's end, Minister Jaro (Frank Langella) had relieved Kira of her duties aboard *DS9* and sent her back to Bajor.

"I remember how Sisko and Kira said goodbye. For all intents and purposes, it was a *real* goodbye. It was an opportunity to show how deep their relationship went," says Vistor. "We got to see Kira in action, being a freedom fighter again."

"The Circle" revealed that, ironically, the Cardassians were responsible for arming the Bajoran freedom fighters and that Jaro is the Circle leader. Kira was kidnapped and beaten, then rescued by Sisko, Li and Bashir. Desperate to convince Bajor's Council of Ministers of the Cardassians' attempts to provoke a Bajoran civil war, Sisko prepared to make one last stand against a Bajoran assault force determined to wrest control of *DS9*.

ROBBIE ROBINSON

One day in Deep Space Nine's *third season, Kira woke up with an alien face. She turned Cardassian for "Second Skin."*

"What I remember most about that episode was that we started to see Kira's romantic side," says Visitor. "Many people were waiting to see that happen, myself included. We showed just a little bit of that with Bareil. Kira started to lose her edge and understand a little bit about spirituality."

Finally, there was "The Siege," which brought the trilogy to a close. Sisko and his team of resisters face off against the Bajoran forces, stalling them long enough for Dax and Kira to gain entrance to the Council. "That was an exciting show. We had our two females, Dax and Kira, going on a mission together in this horrible little Bajoran tin can that barely flew," Visitor recalls. "It was an exciting thing, that there was a pilot, and a co-pilot and both were women. It felt important to do.

"I was basically in the hot seat for all three episodes. It was an incredibly hard working schedule. Everyone seemed to come and go and I remained."

"Necessary Evil" focused on the relationship between Odo and Kira. "It goes back five years," she explains. "I'm this punk freedom fighter and Odo is this very new security officer. We see how the ramifications of what happened then affect us and our relationship now.

"The relationship is left unresolved at the episode's end. I love the fact that they do that on *Deep Space Nine.* You can't just eat your cookies, drink your milk and go to sleep after seeing the show. It keeps you up a bit, makes you think."

Much has been made of the fact that the women on *Deep Space Nine* have far more to do than their *Next Generation* counterparts. Both Gates McFadden and Marina Sirtis were vocal in their efforts to be given more activity aboard the *Enterprise.* Over the years, they say, it paid off. Perhaps the biggest bene-

ficiaries of their efforts have been *Deep Space Nine's* Visitor and Farrell.

"All the women who came before us made a difference in how our roles were designed," notes Visitor. "I've been in relationships where you've tried to get a man to marry you, but he's resisting the relationship. You figure he is just not the marrying kind and you leave him. Two months later, you find out he got married to the next woman he met. That seems to be a common pattern. He needed to be comfortable with [marriage], so he could finally face it in a fresh environment. Maybe, in a sense, that's what happened with *Star Trek.* Marina and all the other women had an effect on what Terry and I get to do on *Deep Space Nine.* And I'm very grateful to them."

Born and raised in New York City by her choreographer father and ballet teacher mother, Visitor began performing at age 14 in school musicals and fell in love with acting. She spurned the chance to attend Princeton in order to be a chorus girl in a stage musical. Parts in plays such as *42nd Street* followed, as did guest starring roles on such TV shows as *Matlock, Empty Nest* and *L.A. Law.* Then came a co-starring role on the short-lived TV version of *Working Girl.*

And, now there is *Deep Space Nine.* About the only elements of her *Trek* experience that Visitor dislikes are the 90-minute process involved in applying Kira's ridged nose and the endless hours spent filming. "It certainly helps me give the character her edge," she says, "but the hours are truly the toughest thing."

As for the makeup, it has led to a few good laughs and what she affectionately refers to as the "doctor story." "I fell coming out of the hair trailer," she explains. "It had rained and I was coming out of the trailer holding an umbrella and walking on these slick, rickety steps. I fell right on the metal steps. I couldn't move, so they took me to a clinic.

"I had gone through makeup and hair, but I was still in street clothes. All the doctor knew was that I had fallen. He walked in with his face in his papers, saying, 'OK, you've fallen.' Just at that point, he glanced up. He yelled, 'My God, your nose!' He thought I fell on my nose and had accordioned it. I could see in this guy's eyes that he was envisioning his name in medical books because of this nose.

"So I said, 'No, no, I'm from *Star Trek.* It's makeup!' He covered with, 'Oh yeah, we get a lot of the *Star Trek* people in here.' He was trying to be *so* cool. Of course, it's a testament to the makeup. It's pretty amazing. In person, you can't tell it's a prosthetic."

Looking to the future, Visitor plans to proudly display that accordion nose for years to come. Major Kira Nerys, she believes, is a part of her now, and a part she looks forward to evolving for as long as *Deep Space Nine* remains in orbit. "I just don't want Kira to lose her edges, to become pabulum. I know through all of my own experiences in life that I've mellowed," concludes Nana Visitor. "I know better about certain things now than I did when I was younger. But I still have my edges and there are still ways to push my buttons. I just want to see Kira evolve truthfully, as a real person would."

THE SAVAGE BEAST

By Marc Shapiro and Ed Gross

Ron Perlman is normally too much of a sweetheart to lay down the law. But, after a trio of films (*Quest for Fire*, *Ice Pirates* and *The Name of the Rose*) in which the veteran actor was only recognizable through his name on the cast list, Perlman called his manager and told him enough was enough.

"I told him I was no longer interested in *any* role in which I would have to wear prosthetic makeup," recalls Perlman. "I told him I didn't want to see *any* scripts with those kinds of roles and I didn't want to be tempted. Fortunately, I have the kind of manager who doesn't always listen to his clients.

"A few days later, I went out to pick up my morning paper and there was this script for something called *Beauty & the Beast* laying next to it. Since the script was lighter than the morning paper, I read it first. I got halfway through it, called my manager and said, 'What do I have to do to play this character?' "

Perlman claims that the idea of spending five hours daily geting into his Beast makeup has a built-in nuisance factor. "Just sitting there can be a real strain. But the quality of the work far overshadows the negatives," he says.

And the quality for Perlman centers on his character, the man-beast Vincent who, he claims, has a range of possibilities for him as an actor to interpret.

"Vincent is a character of incredible sensitivity and compassion. He is a heroic champion of the underdog with incredible inner strength who knows what it's like to have to overcome insurmountable weakness.

"The effect he's allowed to have on this woman and she on him is very poignant and moving. There's *nothing* one-dimensional about Vincent. There are any number of directions this character could go in."

While that may be the case, creator/producer Ron Koslow and his team have kept *Beauty & the Beast* walking a fine line between fairy tale fantasy and gritty urban reality. That believability extends to Vincent's relationship with the lovely Catherine (Linda Hamilton). Perlman chalks that element up to good chemistry between the two actors.

"The reason the relationship rings true is that I have a real affection for Linda," he says. "I find her an incredibly beautiful person and one who possesses a wide range of emotions. Feeling that way about her makes it very easy for Vincent to love Catherine.

"The relationship is not going anywhere. What it is now is what it will *always* be. The ramifications of the relationship are what we are exploring and each episode adds new colors to it. This show is not dealing with a plight or a cause but, rather, with an aspect of humanity that will be explored. Through the actions of Vincent and Catherine, people will know what it is to find true love.

"Vincent *is* the Prince, and the job that [makeup creator] Rick Baker has done, and the job that the writers have done and the job that I'm trying to do, bears that out in every episode," explains Perlman. "He is the most sublime thing in Catherine Chandler's life. He doesn't need to change, to become that Prince, to be accepted by her. That's how we get around the transformation. There's *no reason* to see this guy change because he's as close to perfect as you're going to get."

Perlman is referring to the final moments of the original tale of *Beauty & the Beast* as well as the classic Jean Cocteau live-action film and the animated Disney movie musical in which Beauty's love transforms the homely, but noble Beast into a handsome Prince. The same passion ignites Vincent's relationship with Catherine.

TONY ESPARZA

This is the face of the Beast. Behind the makeup of this most sensitive of heroes is Ron Perlman.

> "Vincent is a character
> of incredible sensitivity
> and compassion,"
> Perlman notes.

TONY ESPARZA

"It's *so* romantic," Perlman enthuses, "and it's not really very science fiction or fantasy-oriented. It's very real and they've managed to find very contemporary equivalents to magical and fanciful elements, but in a very real setting. It's very easy to suspend your disbelief, which is one of the things that I've discovered working on it. The benefits of playing Vincent are incredible. There are elements that one must come to grips with in terms of Vincent's character, which are so elevated, noble and regal, you can't help but get involved in the things that are happening. He's also so spiritual, so sensitive to the world and humanity around him, that I've begun looking at the world through his eyes, because I spend so many hours of my day walking in his shoes.

"I'm not going to say that I've *become* Vincent," he adds. "I don't want you to interpret this in that way, but the only thing an actor has as his tools is his own experience, and you must find things in yourself to play what the character in the script calls for. One of the turn-ons about being an actor is being given the opportunity to occasionally be more or less than you are. It certainly takes you out of the realm of being yourself.

"Vincent has the potential to be a great American folk hero. I wouldn't want to violate the trust that has been placed in my hands by having the character involved in anything cheap or shoddy.

"When people look at Vincent, I want them to see somebody they can have confidence in and trust. They should admire his worldliness and care about the fact that he can alternately be weak and strong."

Perlman, who has seemingly made a career as an actor who dons prosthetics, feels that there is a significant difference between Vincent and his earlier roles in *Quest for Fire* and *The Name of the Rose*.

"The humanity of those two people was so abstract, that I had to form a new level of behavior," he explains. "A new walk a new voice, a new language, new places that the language comes from—those are all intellectual decisions and inventive decisions. Vincent needs to be played right from the heart. It's a role that separates romantic leading characters from character actor roles. I play both now, and Vincent, aside from the fact that he's so physically different, is definitely a romantic hero."

Vincent is quite a distinctive character. "I had played beasts prior to this," Perlman says. "This was not only a beast, but a beast who lived as an extension of his pain every moment of every day, and all of that was there in the relationship with this woman who opened up all of these new feelings in him. It was just mindblowing that somebody could come up with a character that crystallized all of the beasts that had ever been written in history, including the Hunchback of Notre Dame, the beast from the Cocteau film and the beast that I played in *Name of the Rose*. These guys, I always felt, had tremendous feelings underneath their ugliness. I just saw an incredible sensitivity on the part of the writer for this man's pain and his ability to transcend it."

Although his special makeup has its grueling aspects, there are equal compensations. "Makeup has always been rather freeing to me," Perlman admits. "When you're playing a character, you're playing someone other than yourself, and when you physically put something on that makes you look like somebody else, then it frees you to *be* that person. It is, however, something of a nuisance to be sitting in a chair four hours every day to get made up, and then for an hour to get the makeup taken off. I have had more than my fair share of 20-hour days."

Greatly loved by his fans, despite the loss of Catherine in the series' third season, Vincent still possesses a phenomenal appeal. He's a character beloved by Perlman, a lion-man who may yet be reprised, at some point in the future, by Perlman in a film revival plotted by creator Koslow.

In the mysterious world under Manhattan, Father (Roy Dotrice) raised Vincent as his own son.

"There's not a character around that I've come into contact with who possesses as much humility as Vincent does. That humility serves as a backdrop to his other qualities, which are incredible strength, both spiritual and physical, and an innate leadership quality based on his solitude and his aloneness and good judgment, as well as his compassion for the underdog."

As a science-fiction hero, though, there are a couple of seemingly glaring inconsistencies in the character. Is Vincent a human being, an animal or something completely different? And why, when Vincent speaks better English than a Rhodes scholar 90 percent of the time, does he suddenly revert to wild animal screams when provoked by violence?

"Vincent is part man and part beast," Perlman responds. "What his origin is has never been specified. But there is obviously something different about his makeup. Whatever he is, he must possess incredible genes to have both superior intelligence and strength.

"As far as the roaring goes, I think the audience needs some kind of signal that there is this fierce other side to Vincent so they don't get completely hooked on the idea of this creature who speaks perfect English. It keeps the audience just that little bit off-balance."

Says Perlman, "I don't think I'll ever grow tired of playing Vincent."

Perlman was born in Manhattan in 1950. While his early childhood was fairly unaffected, by the time Perlman became a teen he fell victim to some very Vincent-like mental trauma.

"I was not dealt the best physical hand in the world," says a candid Perlman. "My nose didn't fit my mouth. My forehead didn't fit my cheeks. And those are traditionally the years when a boy is judged primarily on his looks. So, consequently, I suffered from very low self-esteem. In a sense, I had a beast inside me. That beast was fear and insecurity."

Perlman tamed that beast in high school, by turning his energies to performing; first as a comedian and later as an actor. After college, he worked on the New York stage, where director Jean-Jacques Annaud hired him to make the stone-age drama *Quest for Fire*. Perlman's memories of portraying a caveman focus on battling hypothermia in the great outdoors and going to zoos to study the movements of apes.

Perlman's next fantastic film assignment was *Ice Pirates*. "Outside of having the opportunity to be in a film with Anjelica Huston, it's a movie I would just as soon forget," winces Perlman. "I'm not ashamed of having done it. It's the results I'm not happy with. The picture had a great deal of promise, but the producers decided to aim real low with it."

Next on Perlman's prosthetic hit parade was *The Name of the Rose*, a mystery set in a monastery. For the role of Salvatore, a facially deformed and hunchbacked monk, it was another hours-a-day stint in a makeup chair. He was happy with the role but he concedes that putting on the makeup in another movie was an ordeal.

"In the space of three films, I had become one of the least recognized actors in the business," says Perlman. "I guess it was largely ego, but I felt, at that point, I could carry a major role *without* hiding my face."

So how given this attitude, does Perlman justify yet another masked man role in *Beauty & the Beast*?

"I really don't look at Vincent as being a makeup role. Vincent is a very real character, one I play honestly and sincerely. He is not a creation from the imagination but rather one from the heart. Vincent is a part I don't think I could grow tired of playing. It's the most beautiful character I've ever played," Ron Perlman says, "and maybe that I ever will."

69

TRUE DISBELIEVER

By Kyle Counts

It isn't that Gillian Anderson doesn't want to talk about acting, she's just so busy working that interviews are rather a luxury these days.

Co-star (with David Duchovny) of *The X-Files*, Anderson is in the middle of yet another long shooting day in Vancouver, British Columbia, where the show is based. She spends five days a week on the set, with Friday's filming stretching well into the wee hours of Saturday morning, meaning that talking about the series takes a back seat to such decadent pursuits as sleeping and caring for her new daughter.

The hazel-eyed, auburn-haired performer seems to have found a perfect match in her *X-Files* role as Special Agent Dana Scully, a doctor recruited out of medical school by the FBI to team up with Special Agent Fox "Spooky" Mulder (Duchovny). Mulder is obsessed with investigating cases outside the Bureau mainstream—things like UFOs, carnivorous human beasts and intelligent computers that kill people, unexplained phenomena relegated to the black hole of FBI archives known as the "X" files. While Mulder is portrayed as an offbeat, open-to-anything psychologist, Anderson's Scully cuts a cool figure as his skeptical, logical-minded counterpart, a woman who is loath to believe what cannot be explained

In an ironic reversal on their characters' attitudes, Anderson believes in the paranormal whereas co-star Duchovny does not.

"As Scully sees more, she develops more of an open mind," Anderson explains. On screen, she is beginning to believe.

scientifically. (A typical exchange between the two: She: "You don't really believe that." He: "Do you have a more credible explanation?")

"It's a great part," Anderson enthuses of her service as a science-fiction heroine. "Scully is strong, she's independent, and she's very smart. It's a very appealing woman's role."

Expounding on the qualities that made Anderson a perfect fit with Dana Scully, series creator Chris Carter says, "Gillian's smart, first of all. And, she's ambitious, which is what her character is. Scully is one of the few women in what is otherwise a very male-dominated institution, the FBI. So, she has to compete with these guys and still maintain a sense of her own femininity, which I think she does very well, both in life and in terms of the character."

Scully mirrors Anderson's own personality in that both share a strong desire to excel in their professions, as well as a tendency to get "completely wrapped up" in their work, the actress says. "The more comfortable I get with my character, the looser she gets, the more she becomes like me. I don't have

an undergraduate degree in physics or a medical degree, and she does—that's a big part of who the character is. She's very analytical, and that's how she approaches everything she does. I don't operate from that 'heady' realm of thinking. I'm more spontaneous."

During high school, Anderson was active in community theater, taking that love of the stage with her to the National Theatre of Great Britain at Cornell University in Ithaca, NY, and then to the Goodman Theatre School at Chicago's DePaul University, where she graduated with a Bachelor of Fine Arts degree.

Getting the lead in a Fox TV series might swell the head of a more ego-driven performer, but Anderson's reaction to her small screen success is rooted in knock-on-wood candor. "If I thought about it too much, it would scare the hell out of me. I'm just taking it as it comes. I guess it's a pretty big deal. I'm very, very lucky. But it's a lot of pressure and a lot of work."

Her audition for *The X-Files* was "basically just another audition like all other auditions, except that I felt very strongly

71

about the script. I love mysteries, and it was written very well. I went through the whole callback process, then went into Fox a couple of times and read with David. It was pretty intense. It was quite a shocking surprise when I got the part."

In the pilot, which concerns the mysterious murders of a group of young adults, all of whom hail from the same 1989 graduating class, Scully asks her boss, Chief Blevins (Charles Cioffi), if she's being sent to team with Mulder in order to "debunk" his work. "Just make the proper scientific analysis," he tells her, sidestepping the question. While she may not realize it, her job—to write field reports on the "validity" of Mulder's findings—is, in fact, part of the Bureau's agenda to downplay her partner's consuming devotion to these bizarre, previously abandoned cases. In that sense, then, is she an unwitting spy for the FBI?

"Originally, that was the premise," Anderson replies. "But Mulder and I have become much more intimate in our work [since then]. We have a great respect for each other and the passion we each have for our own process within that work. It has become much more of a partnership than me just looking out for him, but that's still my job, to oversee the work that he does and to make sure he doesn't go too far."

The fact that Scully doesn't believe in ghosts and goblins makes it easy for her to be skeptical and point out where Mulder is "going wrong." "It makes for a good tension in the show, as well as a good, active relationship in terms of how it plays on screen," Anderson says. "We have different opinions and different beliefs, and different ways of approaching the cases that we come across. Mulder is very loose—he wears these wacky ties—while Scully is obsessive about her work and doesn't really have time to pay attention to fashion. She's a very tight, cool character, very intelligent, very analytical, and very determined to solve these cases and help people."

Fans of *The X-Files* will be fascinated to learn that it is Anderson, and *not* her co-star, who is open to accepting otherworldly phenomena on the order of UFOs and artificial intelligence. "I, Gillian, *do* believe in the paranormal, whereas David does *not*. It's interesting that those roles are reversed [in the show]." How long will Scully continue to remain skeptical, then, being that nearly irrefutable evidence of paranormal activity is being presented to her weekly? "It will be interesting to see how we pull that off from episode to episode," Anderson comments. "There are episodes where she starts to see Mulder's side of things and begins to open up a little more to those realms of possibilities. But she deals with reality and what is tangible. If you look at every episode, there is a *logical* reason for the things that happen."

Anderson praises Duchovny as a "very generous actor. He's very funny and a pleasure to work with. He helped me out a lot in the pilot. Not having had any real experience in front of the camera at all, he was very helpful in teaching me the ropes. We work very well together. Depending on the day and our moods and how tired we are, we either work very freely, very professionally, or we goof around. You need that kind of comic relief sometimes to get through the day."

Considering the straight-faced nature of the character he plays, it's surprising that Anderson considers Duchovny a "funny" actor. "Oh, he's hysterical," she smiles. "Sometimes there are kitschy phrases written into the script that are very similar to his own sense of humor. He adds a lot of humor to the show himself. If you see little jokes, it's more likely than not that he has either added it where it didn't exist or changed something that was there to make it funny."

Anderson emphasizes that there will *never* be a romance between Scully and Mulder. She believes *The X-Files* is a positive role model in that it demonstrates men and women can work alongside one another without sex becoming an issue between them. "In today's times, I think it's very important that [men and women] learn to work together and to develop intellectually stimulating relationships. You can be attracted to somebody, but that doesn't mean you have to act on it. You can get to know a person intimately without having to consummate the relationship."

In real life, Anderson did find romance on *The X-Files* with one of the series' key creative personnel, marrying art director Clyde Klotz. The couple have a daughter, Piper, requiring some innovative second season storylines to "hide" Anderson's pregnancy. In fact, the "X" Files division was even closed down on the show, then eventually reopened.

Of *The X-Files* explored thus far, Anderson counts two among her favorites. "As an actress, my favorite one for a long time was 'Squeeze,' the one about the 300-year-old man who goes into hibernation and kills five people every 30 years and rips their livers out. 'Ice' has replaced that as my favorite. I feel that my work in it is my strongest thus far, and it's very well-written. It takes place in Alaska, and it's very similar to *The Thing*. The FX are great."

Overall, Anderson says it's the professional challenge that makes her association with *The X-Files* so rewarding. "It's challenging as an actor to find ways to improve my craft. I'm constantly working with new scripts, and the amount of people I get to meet and work with is wonderful too. But it's most rewarding in terms of what I'm learning as an actor. The hardest thing is the hours and the amount of time we put in. Sometimes, depending on the episode, we work 16-hour days back to back. It's hard because it can be exhausting. And it's hard to show up for scripts that I'm not crazy about. But when good scripts come along, it's just a delight."

Response to *The X-Files* continues to grow, with the show emerging as a bona fide hit in its second season. No actor can ever predict how long a series will run, of course, but Gillian Anderson is perhaps more pragmatic than most about her hopes for the program. "I hope the show goes as long as it needs to go. If it starts getting stale, there are enough people watching for that to pull it back in. We have some very creative people working on *The X-Files*, and I foresee it going for a while. We're slowly getting a very strong following. If it goes as long as it needs to go, that'll be enough for me."

DINOSAUR HUNTRESS

By Bill Warren

Until summer 1993, Laura Dern was known principally as one of the best actresses of her generation, with fine performances in movies like *Smooth Talk*, *Afterburn*, *Blue Velvet* and *Rambling Rose* (for which she received an Oscar nomination). But with one film, she has become a lithe-limbed, two-fisted science-fiction heroine—because she is, of course, Dr. Ellie Sattler in Steven Spielberg's *Jurassic Park*, the largest-grossing movie *ever made*. She took the leap from drama to adventure for several reasons, with one in particular.

"Steven asked me to," she says with a typically warm grin. "I had heard rumors as it was being cast that Steven and [producer] Kathleen Kennedy were thinking very seriously about me doing it, so when the offer came, I wasn't surprised.

"We met and talked about the part. Steven looked at me and said, 'You're not getting an Academy Award for this one, and filming may be a nightmare half the time, but I think you'll have a lot of fun, and I really think you should do this.' From that point on, we had a blast." Her real delight in making *Jurassic Park* is obvious in her entertaining performance. Even though she's persuasively scared and plays the dramatic scenes with conviction, she's clearly having a ball.

For one thing, she loved working with Spielberg. "He has an *amazing* imagination and amazing courage. Being a little boy himself in his imagination, there are no boundaries, no 'That's not possible'—he takes off not only as a filmmaker, but as a visionary. Steven creates a world people wouldn't believe in otherwise. He's very funny and very charming; I had a very good relationship with him.

"Some of his characters are sometimes much larger than life—so are David Lynch's, actually," she says, referring to *Wild at Heart* and *Blue Velvet*, the two movies she made with Lynch. "Steven and David share a real macabre

sense of comedy and style, even though they're completely different. They like being, not camp, but larger than life. And there is some of that in *Jurassic*.

"I'm sure *Jurassic Park* will be the only movie of this nature I'll ever do," Dern suggests, "but I loved doing it. Ordinarily, I love pieces in which you can get inside people's emotions, and things like that. This was completely different from that; like

TRADEMARK & COPYRIGHT 1993 UNIVERSAL CITY STUDIOS & AMBLIN ENTERTAINMENT

"Should kids see Jurassic Park?*" Dern asks. "To me, it's scary, fun, imaginative. It's an adventure."*

Special FX created the spectacular denizens of Jurassic Park. And Dern had no trouble in believing them to be real.

MURRAY CLOSE

Jaws, it's the kind of movie where Steven cared about the people and the characters and didn't want the emphasis to just be on the creatures. I think that's why most of Steven's movies have been so loved, because E.T., Close Encounters and Jaws were as much about the people as anything."

In Jurassic Park, Ian Malcolm (Jeff Goldblum) flirts with Dern's Ellie Sattler, and at one point, she reveals, "we shot even

more of that, of his 'pursuit' of my character. But what is in there now is really the perfect amount; Steven was correct to cut what he did, because otherwise it would have been a kind of caricature of this smarmy guy going after another guy's girl. Now, he asks about me in the car, and Sam [Neill as Alan Grant] nukes it in the bud."

She wound up sold on Goldblum herself; Dern freely ad-

With Richard Attenborough and Sam Neill, Dern watched a truly unique event: the birth of a baby dinosaur.

mits that she and Goldblum are "sweethearts" because of meeting on the set. And she likes his acting, too.

"I loved working with Jeff; he's hilarious and charming, and an amazing actor. I'm not someone who has crushes per se, but I love creative, talented people. I've always gone out with people who are artists on some level; I'm really fascinated by that, be it an actor, writer, director or whatever.

"But it was easy to love all the people on *Jurassic Park* because they're amazing. Richard Attenborough is the most wonderful, charming, gracious, sweet man I've ever had the pleasure to work with. And Sam Neill—he's just the best. These are great people. But Jeff, in my opinion, steals the movie.

"Being part of the movie and watching his work, and watching Sam's work, and all the guys, you can't help but love them. And I love Malcolm, too, because he's the [film's] sense of humor, and also its conscience. One of my favorite lines is 'What you call discovery, I call the rape of the natural world.' I think the comment that he makes about this side of science is a very important one for people to hear, because *Jurassic Park* isn't just a dinosaur movie, it's also a movie that says maybe we should have our greatest minds finding a cure for AIDS and working out efficient forms of solar energy before we get into cloning for greed."

Dern was delighted with *Jurassic Park* when she finally saw it,

finding it as scary as anyone else in the audience. "It was scary for me sometimes as the actor, too, and as the character. Very exciting, challenging things happen. But the thing that's so exciting to me, that interested me in the book—and in Michael Crichton's writing generally—is that it is not just the adventure that's scary. The process of the cloning and regeneration of things that are extinct is also terrifying. Scientists playing God is certainly as scary as a dinosaur coming around the corner. So there's a kind of double whammy."

Jurassic Park wasn't only a kind of movie that Dern hasn't done before, it gave her the opportunity to do things on screen she never had, such as action scenes. "I enjoyed that, because I've never been athletic in a movie, and I enjoy athletics. Running and jumping, and doing all that wild stuff—I had a good time. But there were a lot of minor ailments and bruises and muscle tears. Usually, it's emotional exhaustion I feel at the end of a movie; this was completely the opposite.

"Riding a bone for 10 hours can really bruise you up. The thought of me hanging off that skeleton! I remember hanging from this thing, then it was three hours later, and it's digging in. I didn't want to get down because I was too lazy to keep getting back on the thing, so there's this giant bruise on my thigh, swelling, because I'm hanging on so long. I was hanging upside down with Kathy Kennedy laughing and going, 'You're hanging from a bone—and you're a serious actress.' I never expected my career to get to that point," she laughs.

Dern spends much of her time with actors, freely admitting, "I love actors. People say they're this or that, but I've grown

"Scientists playing God is certainly as scary as a dinosaur coming around the corner," says Dern.

up around them, and I enjoy them so much." She's in a good position to know a great deal about actors, since she's the daughter of two Hollywood veterans, Bruce (*Silent Running*) Dern and Diane (*Carnosaur*) Ladd.

Working with Spielberg on *Jurassic Park* crystallized a growing interest of Dern's. "I have interests in directing," she says, "which have just sprouted in the past year or so. It was great to watch the process of something being created that not only had I never watched being created, but which has never been created before. The stuff that Industrial Light & Magic is doing has never been done; being part of the process was really amazing. The different camera techniques, and what as an actor I could and could not do—it was history in the making. Every time movies advance it's exciting to me, because I was

raised around them." In fact, after completing *Jurassic Park*, Dern did direct a short film.

This aspect of making the movie turned out differently than Dern expected. "What I thought would be the most difficult part of making it was reacting in terror to something that wasn't there. But that was remedied by the fact that there *were* things there much of the time, and that made it a lot easier. I thought that was probably going to be really difficult and probably unpleasant—but it was *fantastic*. It was fun to be part of filmmaking in a different way—learning *their* processes, and FX processes in general. I usually don't get to hear about what the filmmaker is up to. But here I had more time to be on that side, and to learn and listen," says Laura Dern with a cheerful smile. "I'm very happy to have been part of *Jurassic Park*."

STARFLEET SIREN

By Brian Lowry and Ian Spelling

After almost 30 years in the familiar role of Commander Uhura, the *U.S.S. Enterprise* communications officer who forever seemed to have one hand clasped to an earringed lobe, Nichelle Nichols gropes for a way to communicate why she has been the object of such adulation from *Star Trek* fans.

Characteristically, when discussing the role, the actress speaks of Uhura, not herself. "The quality of Uhura's character was such that you could admire her on the one hand as a woman of strength, courage and compassion, and yet she was a *female* female," Nichols suggests.

"I mean, she had legs and boobs and high cheekbones and a little waistline and different hairdos. I don't think she's diminished by a short skirt, boots and jade earrings."

Might we, then, simply attribute Uhura's appeal to a healthy dose of good old-fashioned, down-to-Earth lust? "I hope so," Nichols responds quickly, bursting into laughter. "Oh Lord, I hope so."

Lounging in her home near Los Angeles, the trappings of the series—and many of the opportunities it provided—are ever-present. Replicas of both the *Enterprise* and the Space Shuttle dot her mantleplace, the latter a reminder of her important work as a recruiter for NASA, the only case on record of a real science-fiction heroine actually recruiting others to be real heroes.

For the most part, however, Nichols' life with *Star Trek* has been a bold journey all its own in keeping with her irrepressible energy. There's the constant demand for personal appearances, acting, singing and charitable work. And, of course, there are the six *Star Trek* films in which Nichols has appeared.

The unusual leap from small screen to big screen, Nichols admits, did create problems. "It was difficult with the first film, and it showed," she contends. "There was a stiffness, I thought, and a complication with the script, which was stilted.

"In retrospect, I find *Star Trek: The Motion Picture* most interesting, which I didn't the first time out, because it wasn't *Star Trek*. But as a science fiction entity and a work of art, it's incredible. In *Star Trek II, III* and *IV*, they went back to the *Star Trek* formula that Gene Roddenberry created in the first place. It has gotten better and better and more *us*."

Looking back, Nichols thinks the crucial moment in the film series came after Spock's death. "That almost blew the whole thing apart," she confides. "You know, Leonard Nimoy wanted out, so they accommodated him.

"Paramount didn't really know if they were going to do another *Star Trek*. The fact they were doing *Star Trek II* was a phenomenon. They were shocked by the amount of interest and support out there. What they didn't account for is that this is not just fans from 20 years ago who are 20 years older and holding onto nostalgia. These nuts have raised their kids on it!

"There's a whole new generation of brilliant little darlings, raised on the philosophies of *Star Trek*. And think what that is: non-interference; peaceful exploration; infinite diversity in infinite combinations; you're somebody *because* of your differences, not *in spite* of your differences."

As part of Star Trek *in the '60s, Nichols inspired such young fans as Mae Jemison (later a real-life astronaut) and Whoopi Goldberg.*

According to Nichols, the "Spock trilogy" of Star Trek II-IV *successfully returned to Gene Roddenberry's original* Trek *formula.*

The *Star Trek* principles, the actress argues, have as much validity now as when Roddenberry framed them. "I don't want anybody being color-blind when they look at me. I resent somebody saying, 'Oh, I don't mind that she's black, I'm color-blind.' Well, wake up, fella, and smell the roses.

"I *like* being who I am, and I'll be damned if I watch you accepting me in *spite* of the fact that I'm a woman and I'm black and I'm whoever I am. Deal with me, and appreciate and accept me for what I am.

"That's what *Star Trek* said is right and is the way to go. We took off from Earth with the understanding that whatever we saw out there was going to be different from what we are, and to accept it."

After all these years, Nichols still has a great deal of affection for the *Star Trek* saga. "I still have that personal attachment and proprietorship, as though it were my baby. And it is, each and every one of ours.

"That's what made it so good. No matter what our interpersonal relationships at a given time—the show came first. We could set aside any petty differences for that show. At least, I felt we did, and I know *I* did.

"That's part of *Star Trek*'s secret of success. Each and every person in it felt a dedication to their character. That became the truth and sparkle, the *Star Trek* reality."

Star Trek V: The Final Frontier, Nichols comments, lacked a quality story and worse, had a misguided, muddled message. These faults, she feels, were responsible for its relatively poor box-office performance and the general sense of disappointment expressed by most *Trek* fans.

"I thought it wasn't a good story. You go in search of God, and if you don't find yourself, what the hell are you going to find? What they came up with," she decides, "was a bit of a sham, a cop-out. If you won't make a statement on who or what God is, then why do it?"

Much to Nichols' surprise, William Shatner made a game effort in his directorial debut. "He was better than I thought he would be. He's a lot better working with as a director than he is as an actor," she notes candidly.

Many *Trek* devotees didn't appreciate watching the supporting cast play off their reputations for easy laughs. At least one *Trek* actor, George Takei, made it clear that he felt "mocked" when Sulu and Chekov (Walter Koenig) got lost, or when Scotty (James Doohan) bumped his head seconds after boasting how well he knew the ship. Takei also believes that Uhura had been exploited in a scene which called for her to dance provocatively on a hilltop to provide a distraction.

The actress, however, dismisses such talk. "Oh, I think George is a little overboard there. As far as I'm concerned, those

JOHN SHANNON/COPYRIGHT 1984 PARAMOUNT PICTURES CORP.

are some of the charming moments in a failed film. I wouldn't have done it if I felt it would be demeaning," she says. "I liked Uhura dancing up there with the two moons behind her."

Nichols also enjoyed the sly flirtations she shared with Scotty. "Wasn't that fun?" she asks. "I decided, since there's nothing between Scotty and Uhura romantically, to play it from the same point-of-view that Nichelle has with Jimmy Doohan. We're very good friends, and we joke around and play kissy-pooh. We couldn't take it any further than we did, you know, because it's really just *inconceivable*. It just doesn't happen. But, it *was* fun and the fans loved it."

As for *Star Trek VI: The Undiscovered Country,* "the film has what I feel is an important message. I saw it the minute I read the script. *Trek VI* is really about getting in touch with our own prejudices, even though we might think we've come a long way and see beyond such personal prejudices," she explains. "At some point, we all really have them, and we have to deal with them because life changes and we have to change with it. It was a good story with an excellent message. Nick Meyer did a fine job [as director]. He was working with two other directors [Nimoy and Shatner]. He got what he wanted, and I think *Star Trek VI* is truly a Nick Meyer film."

Fans the world over recognize the actress. Many Trekkers willingly stand on line for hours to secure her autograph and a friendly word at her frequent convention appearances. Nichols is, in a word, adored. "You don't get that with just a few 'Hailing frequencies open.' We did TV's first interracial kiss and the episode with Abraham Lincoln ["The Savage Curtain"]. When Uhura was involved, they really cracked a mold. Dr. Martin Luther King once told me, 'You've opened a door that can never be closed again. You've changed the face of television.' That," Nichols happily notes, "is no small achievement. And I am very, very proud.

"*Star Trek* made sweeping statements about society and relationships between people at the same time Captain Kirk swashbuckled. We *never* lost sight of the first law of show business: To entertain. We did it and made our statements without preaching. That's what Gene Roddenberry intended to accomplish when he specifically cast George Takei and me on the command crew. And he did it.

"That's why I rather resent it when people say Uhura didn't do anything but say, 'Hailing frequencies open.' That's *not true.* It demeans my status. Uhura represented womanhood and the breakthrough of cross-racial representation. She represented dignity and intelligence, and no one can take that away from her, or me."

An accomplished singer, Nichols has toured with her one-woman show, *Reflections* (in which she portrays many of the legends who inspired her, Sarah Vaughan, Billie Holiday and others), recorded albums (*Nichelle: Songs from the Galaxy* on CD from Crescendo Records) and penned her autobiography, *Beyond Uhura* (Putnam, 1994).

And now, after 29 years of boldly going where no one has gone before, if her ongoing *Star Trek* journey has really come to an end, Nichols will simply thank her lucky stars, and the fans.

"Twenty-nine years. It seems impossible, doesn't it? It's wondrous and marvelous, phenomenal and incredible. It has been truly unbelievable. I find myself having the best time of my life. If you said to me 29 years ago, 'You'll be doing this in some way for 29 years,' I would probably have said, "Twenty-nine years? I won't even be able to move, much less act, sing and dance.' And you know what? Here I am doing it, and I'm having more fun and more success than when I started out.

"I owe that to the fans. I've always said, more than a fan of *Star Trek*—and I love the philosophy of *Star Trek* and what Gene Roddenberry set out to achieve—I'm a fan of the fans. I love them. They're fabulous. I love being around them. I love their madness and their caring. I love watching them take off for a weekend, don the costumes, and become characters from the 23rd century and beyond. I thank the fans for giving us—me—so much support, and love.

"I want them to know I love them. They'll always be my friends. I'll see the fans, always," promises Nichelle Nichols. "They can rest assured of that."

79

MASTER OF THE TIME MACHINE

By Steve Swires

Two decades before Mel Gibson and Nicole Kidman made it fashionable to be Australian, Rod Taylor was the first Aussie actor to become a major Hollywood star since Errol Flynn. Taylor earned a permanent place in the pantheon of science-fiction heroes for his thoughtful performances in two genre classics, George Pal's wondrous *The Time Machine* and Alfred Hitchcock's chilling *The Birds*.

"I've been such a phony American for so many years that most people have forgotten I'm really Australian," the outspoken actor acknowledges. "I must have a lucky imitative ear. It certainly has nothing to do with talent. I just fell in love with the States as soon as I stepped off the airplane, and set out to become a real American."

Born in Sydney, Australia on January 11, 1929, Taylor originally trained to become a painter, attending the Sydney Technical and Fine Arts College. Inspired by a performance by Sir Laurence Olivier, who was touring Australia with his Old Vic repertory company, Taylor dabbled in amateur dramatics while working for a department store, creating and painting backdrops for fashion displays.

"There I was in a smock surrounded by all the other window dressers," he remembers. "I used to listen to these awful Australian soap operas on the radio. I thought: 'I bet *I* could do that.' So, I went in and auditioned for a soap opera, and was quite well received. I slowly gave up my painting and sketching, and started hanging around coffee shops and pubs pretending I was an actor. Before I knew it, I was."

A busy radio player, Taylor made his domestic screen debut in *The Stuart Expedition*, and played supporting roles in two more Australian films, *King of the Coral Sea* and the Hollywood-financed *Long John Silver*. Anxious to expand his career, he willingly left his native country—and its limited acting opportunities—in 1954.

"Fortunately, *Long John Silver* gave me the break I needed," he explains. "I played the 85-year-old, blind Israel Hands, and I was a little *too* convincing. A message came through from the distributor, Warner Bros.: 'You must get that

Hi-tech espionage was the game when Taylor co-starred with Kirstie Alley and Greg Evigan in another short-lived TV series, Masquerade.

"Kids today remember me more for The Time Machine *than anything else I've ever done," says Taylor.*

old man over to Hollywood. He'll be nominated for a Best Supporting Actor Oscar.'

"I accepted Warner Bros. invitation to come to Hollywood. The studio sent some people to meet the man at the airport, but when they saw this 25-year-old, broken-nosed ex-pug get off the plane, wearing a tight tweed suit, their faces fell. I told them: 'Well, I'm going to stick around, and see if I can *act* my way into this business.' "

Undaunted by this case of mistaken identity, Taylor persevered until he made his American film debut with a bit part in 1955's *The Virgin Queen*. After small roles in *Hell on Frisco Bay* and *Giant*, he secured his first significant supporting part in Edward (*Queen of Outer Space*) Bernds' grade B science fiction flick *World Without End* in 1956. Taylor portrayed an astronaut accidentally thrust into Earth's 26th century, where he and Hugh (*The Day the Earth Stood Still*) Marlowe aided the peaceful human survivors of nuclear holocaust in their war against killer mutants.

"I was so thrilled to have a sizable role in an American movie," Taylor says. "It gave me the confidence to know that I could work with established Hollywood professionals and come out maybe equally as well. I would have taken *any* part,

as long as it was in an American movie. I would have doubled as the *monster*, just to get into the picture."

Eager to please, Taylor bravely battled a pathetically phony giant spider nesting in a cave. "It was a *ridiculous* looking thing," he laughs. "But I dove into it, and wrestled with it for all I was worth. I even made a major creative contribution to that scene. I ad libbed that I was *vomiting* when I came out of the cave, because it was a such a horrific experience with that bunch of rubber and felt."

Screen tested by MGM for the role of boxer Rocky Graziano in *Somebody Up There Likes Me*, Taylor lost out to Paul Newman, but was signed to a long-term studio contract. As part of his contractual commitment to MGM, Taylor appeared on *The Twilight Zone* in 1959. In "And When the Sky Was Opened," written by Rod Serling from a short story by Richard Matheson, he portrayed one of three doomed astronauts who return from the first manned space flight to discover that their existence has been irrevocably extinguished.

"It was an excellent little episode," Taylor states. "It was beautifully written, and it flowed perfectly. I didn't get to meet Serling while I was shooting it, though. I finally met him about 10 years later, when I was a fairly big movie star. He was a dear, sweet guy, and we became good social friends. Naturally, he liked to remind me that I had once done one of his TV shows."

His servitude as a supporting actor completed, Taylor advanced to leading man status in George Pal's adaptation of H.G. Wells' science-fiction novel, *The Time Machine*. "Kids today remember me more from TV reruns of that movie than for anything else I've ever done," he marvels. "I expected it would be a tremendously impressive picture, but I *never* thought it would become a classic."

Although Pal had previously considered Paul (*A Man for All Seasons*) Scofield, Michael (*The Day the Earth Stood Still*) Rennie and James (*20,000 Leagues Under the Sea*) Mason for the demanding role of the intrepid time traveler, he ultimately preferred Taylor's more youthful appeal. For his part, the ambitious actor immediately warmed to the imaginative Hungarian-born filmmaker, whose distinguished track record included *Destination Moon*, *When Worlds Collide* and *War of the Worlds*.

"George Pal was a *genius*," Taylor declares. "He was a lovely, warm-hearted man. I thought of him as a funny little elf. He was surrounded by tiny pup pets and toys, which he brought to life in his movies."

A childhood fan of H.G. Wells' work, Taylor was extremely enthusiastic about his first starring role. "George specifically asked MGM for me," he recounts. "We had lunch several times and discussed the project. He had a marvelous talent for illustration, and I was fascinated with his pre-production drawings. He knew that I was an artist, so we got along beautifully. We worked in close partnership, and I even helped him find the female lead."

Selecting the right actress to play Taylor's love interest, the Eloi maiden Weena, proved to be particularly difficult for Pal. His choice of the inexperienced Yvette Mimieux was initially rejected by MGM.

"There was a *lot* of trouble casting Weena," Taylor affirms. "I suggested that I test with different girls. *My* first choice was Shirley Knight. Yvette and I have since become dear friends, but at that time, I thought she was kind of a strange little hippie child.

"I knew when I did her screen test that Yvette couldn't act at all. But she had a sulky quality which George believed was right. The innocence she projected as part of her character was actually innate in her own personality. I often wondered if she was even listening to me when we shot our scenes.

"Eventually, though, Yvette became a very good actress. She was a delight to work with when we made *Dark of Sun* in 1968. She is actually a much better actress than she is given credit for being."

Paying tribute to the visionary British

That's Taylor wrestling with the "pathetically phony giant spider" in the 1956 low-budget SF flick *World Without End*.

writer, Pal subtly indicated that the time traveler was actually Wells himself by attaching an engraved plate on the time machine which read: "Manufactured by H. George Wells."

"I didn't attempt to think what Wells may have really been like," Taylor comments. "I played *my* version of what a magnificent guy he must have been. Why couldn't he have been strong, romantic and athletic, as well as a brilliant scientist? George was very happy with my conception. I think it was the *ballsiness* of Wells, as I played him, combined with his being highly intellectual, which sold the character."

Rallying the helpless Eloi in a war of liberation, Taylor performed all his own stunts in a strenuous fight scene with their misshapen Morlock oppressors. "Those poor bastards had a *hell* of a time," he chuckles. "They were actually stuntmen wearing rubber Morlock suits, and they were sweating bullets. By the time we finished throwing punches, they were totally exhausted. But it wasn't as dangerous a scene as it looked. What appeared to be high cavern walls and ledges only rose about eight feet in the studio."

Surprised by the unexpected critical and commercial success of *The Time Machine*, Taylor and Pal intended to team up again. Although he turned down the lead role of another heroic scientist in Pal's *The Power* in 1967 (eventually played by George Hamilton), Taylor agreed to star in a subsequent fantasy project, whose title he has since forgotten. "It could have been a magnificent film," he believes. "It was slightly futuristic. I would have played a strange, extremely powerful Howard Hughes type of character in Las Vegas. Unfortunately, George could never get the picture off the ground."

Such disappointment and frustration continually plagued Pal during his final years, even sabotaging his long-planned *Time Machine* sequel, in which Taylor and Mimieux would have reprised their original roles. "George wasn't quite sure what the plot was going to be," Taylor reveals. "He had some marvelous ideas, but he kept changing the concept. He told me about five different storylines, but I never read any completely finalized script." In 1992, Taylor briefly reprised his role in a made-for-video short *The Time Machine Returns*.

Unbeknownst to most of his fans, Taylor has another significant genre credit. He contributed the British accented voice of Pongo, the lead dalmatian, for Walt Disney's 1961 animated classic *101 Dalmatians*.

"Walt had liked me in something, and personally called me to do *101 Dalmatians*," Taylor recounts. "I had forgotten all about it, until it was re-released. Frankly, I've never even seen the film. But Walt was the sweetheart of all time. He and his peo-

ple were so well organized, it was unbelievable. They showed me rough cartoons before I recorded my lines, and I found it fascinating."

Following a brief sojourn into television, (where his series starring work would eventually include *Hong Kong, Bearcats, Masquerade* and *Outlaws*), Taylor returned to the fantasy field, playing a resourceful lawyer confronting the menace of nature inexplicably gone mad in Alfred Hitchcock's *The Birds*.

Striving to achieve the maximum in suspense, Hitchcock frequently put his cast in actual peril, surrounding them with thousands of potentially lethal live birds. "Hitch wanted what he wanted, and he would get it any way he could," Taylor remarks. "Personally, it didn't really bother me. I even volunteered to do the shots of me reaching to close the shutter while the seagulls bit my arm. I took a tetanus shot, and let the seagulls actually bite me, because that was the best way to do the scene.

"But poor Tippi Hedren had a nervous breakdown doing the scene in which she was attacked by birds in the attic. They put her in a corner, and kept throwing so many live birds at her that she went apeshit. And it was no picnic for any of us shooting the scene with the bullfinches flying down out of the chimney. There were more than 1,000 real bullfinches, and they were scared. Do you know what 1,000 bullfinches do when they're scared? They *crapped* all over us."

Relishing the technical challenge of coping with the dictatorial director, Taylor nevertheless considers *The Birds* to be one of Hitchcock's *lesser* achievements. "The movie's first half is almost entirely expository, and I thought that was very bad," he maintains. "I don't know why Hitch spent so much time setting up character relationships that went nowhere. I found the dialogue to be stilted and dull. I didn't think the characters were attractive or interesting people. I especially hated *my* character—a square, repressed idiot who would never have attracted a sophisticated woman like Tippi Hedren. I did everything I could to make him appealing, but it was very difficult."

Today, durable hero Rod Taylor looks back with fondness and pride at his twin journeys into classic science-fiction cinema, aboard *The Time Machine* and beneath *The Birds*.

"When people use the word 'classic' to describe two of my movies, it really makes me feel that my career has been worthwhile," he reflects. "It's wonderful to know that my work has touched so many people. The trip over from Australia in 1954 was definitely worth it. But I wonder whatever became of that damn tweed suit?"

TIME TRIPPER

By Lee Goldberg and Marc Shapiro

When teenager Marty McFly took a wacky scientist's modified DeLorean on a drive, he traveled 30 years into the past. When Michael J. Fox did it, he went back just six weeks.

Back to the Future, the story of Marty's jaunt to the 1950s, had already been shot once—with Eric (*The Fly II*) Stoltz as the star. But six weeks into shooting, director Robert Zemeckis and the film's producers dismissed Stoltz.

And turned back the clock. They started the film again, from scratch. Fox had been considered for the part the first time around but was passed over due to his commitment to *Family Ties*. The catch was still there.

This time, though, the producers didn't care if Fox had to divide his energies between *Family Ties* and *Back to the Future*. He was right for the role—and with a release date looming, they didn't have time to search for second-best.

Executive producer Steven Spielberg passed along a copy

of the *Back to the Future* screenplay to his friend, *Family Ties* producer Gary David Goldberg.

"I went up to Gary's office and he gave me this script and said, 'They're going to call you tomorrow,' " Fox explains. "He had set up with Steven that it would be copacetic with him if I did both the series and the movie."

Fox was excited, but was "really afraid" his performances would suffer from the pressure of doing both at once. "But what could I do? I wasn't going to say, 'Gee Steve, I'm bushed.' You *don't* turn a Steven Spielberg movie down."

It was a torturous schedule. Fox worked on the series during the day and *Back to the Future* at night "and I also had a job at a 7-11 in the Valley," he jokes. "It was intense. Managing time just got insane. I got four hours of sleep a night. But I just toughed it through. The positive way to look at the challenge was to say, 'I'll be very conscious to *not* let the pressure affect my work.' It may have, though."

He didn't give any thought to replacing another actor and doing scenes everyone else on the set had lived through before. "I just looked at it as a fresh job," he says.

Yet, the spirit of the previous shooting was felt. "I would wince a little when someone would suggest where to put the camera and someone else would say, 'Last time we did this scene . . .' "

Following *Back to the Future*'s phenomenal success, Fox, Christopher Lloyd, Zemeckis and writer Bob Gale reunited to continue the story in two further *Future* films, shot back to back. The first sequel took them to the past and the future

"Whatever Doc Brown says, goes, and Marty follows," explains Fox.

The final—for now—film adventure took Lloyd and Fox back to the Old West for a mixture of science fiction and six-guns.

while the second sent Marty McFly and Doc Brown (Lloyd) to the Wild West of the 1800s.

"When it got to the point where I found myself starting to get a little crazed, I would think about things at home and that would balance things out. Doing these films has been a much more comfortable situation than I had *any* idea it would be. I will admit that finding out we would film *II* and *III* at the same time was a surprise. It has been an incredible amount of time to devote to these films. But given the quality of what we've got here, there was never a question that I would do it."

Fox's efforts were made that much more bearable by the fact that Marty Mc-Fly revealed new flaws in the second and third adventures.

"Marty has developed more of an Achilles' heel," says Fox. "In the first film, Marty was more of an unwitting pawn who was just thrown into the situations. He's that way initially in the second, but we came up with a weakness in his personality that stirs the pot and makes things a little worse than they could be.

"He believes in an innocent way that a little manipulation of time will just help him out and who's gonna know? We also explore another flaw in Marty—his unwillingness to back down from confrontation. That facet of Marty thickens the plot and makes him more at the crux of the dilemma. I'm having a lot of fun playing a character with these weaknesses.

"The opportunity to work with Bob [Zemeckis] again was something I jumped at. He's unique, brilliant and totally energizing. He gets everybody pumped up and just gets things done."

He also, laughs Fox, "Put one hell of a strain on my brittle old bones.

"These films are definitely physical. The way Bob is shooting, it almost always *has* to be me in all these wild stunts and not a stunt double, so I'm getting quite a workout. I'm doing some wild stuff which I love to do but, hey, I'm five years older than when I did the last film, and jumping over moving cars and hanging from rafters is starting to take its toll. I'm feeling it a bit more in the morning."

Everyone involved in the making of the *Back to the Future* films invariably makes the point that the movies wouldn't have been made if Michael J. Fox hadn't been lured into a repeat performance as a science-fiction hero. Fox concedes that "it would be hard to make these films without me" but he denies that his appearance is the result of anything other than a creative decision.

"I'm a well-known, well-documented paranoid," says Fox. "I don't take *anything* for granted. Whatever kind of power and clout I may have in this industry is a gun I prefer to keep locked up."

Of his feelings about the place the *Back to the Future* films hold in his working life, Fox notes, "It's very rare in this business that you can have a success in your life that doesn't exact a certain price. I've been lucky enough to have two wonderful

Looking Back to the Future *in 1985, Michael J. Fox and Christopher Lloyd had no idea that their tomorrow included two more movies, a cartoon and a Universal Studio Tour attraction.*

One of five children of an Army officer and a payroll clerk, Fox dropped out of high school to play a 10-year-old in the Canadian TV series, *Leo and Me*. A small role in *Letters From Frank*, a TV movie shot in Vancouver starring Art Carney, led to queries from Hollywood agents. He moved to Hollywood when he was 18 and landed roles in Walt Disney's *Midnight Madness* and guest-shots on *Palmerstown USA*, *Lou Grant*, and *Family*. Between TV appearances, however, Fox sold his furniture to keep the cash flowing and ate more than his share of macaroni and cheese. Then, he was cast as Alex P. Keaton in *Family Ties*, which became the hit TV sitcom that propelled Fox to fame.

Marty McFly's adventures through time are continuing in cartoon form (now on videocassette from MCA Home Video), but Fox is almost certain three live-action movies are enough for him.

"I think everybody envisioned *Back to the Future* as a trilogy, a wonderful way to bring great characters and a great story full circle. If it isn't, the next time I play Marty McFly, it will be in prosthetics. A fourth film is, at best, unlikely. You can only go back to the well so many times. You attempt to go back a fourth or fifth time and it's questionable what you're going to come up with.

"Besides, these three stories are all connected. It would be impossible for a fourth one to connect, so we would have to create something totally different. At that point, everybody would be guessing, and that could be real dangerous."

If there is another round of time travel, the question of age would be a concern. Michael J. Fox has a good laugh at the notion of a thirtysomething actor playing a science-fiction hero pushing 18.

"The age difference is something you just deal with as an actor. Obviously, a 32-year old guy would not sit in a car and say, 'OK, Doc, whatever you say.' He would say, 'Are you *nuts*?' But that's the fun part about playing a character like Marty and doing a picture like *Back to the Future*. Whatever Doc says, goes, and Marty follows. That's the fun part. I get to just suspend belief and go back to being a kid."

work experiences in *Family Ties* and *Back to the Future* that did not require a pound of flesh. I would relive the *Family Ties* period of my life in a second, and it was real easy to say yes to *Back to the Future*. The constant work kept me from mentally getting myself on a lofty perch. After all, the stardom is not what's important. Continuing to work is."

Fox's first film venture into the fantastic was *Teen Wolf*. "I did not do it for any other reason except to be a werewolf. Most people advised me not to do the movie, but that's why I did it."

QUANTUM LEAPER

By Ian Spelling and Marc Shapiro

Quantum Leap came across my agent's desk and then to me," recalls Scott Bakula. "I liked the material so much I just said, 'Let's do it!' "

As a result of that simple decision, Bakula spent the better part of four years leaping in and out of people of all kinds. In his adventures, he's aided, abetted and annoyed by Al (Dean Stockwell), his partner in Project: Quantum Leap, who now projects himself to Beckett [Bakula] via holographic imagery. The premise and the two main figures remained constants; the stories and time periods changed with every episode.

To delve too deeply into *Quantum Leap* would destroy the fun. Scientist Beckett attempted to play with time, time found out, got mad and got even. "Once you can get beyond that and realize we're not dealing with fancy spaceships and all kinds of gadgets, *Quantum Leap* really becomes, in many ways, a simple show," suggests the St. Louis-born Bakula.

Beckett has leaped into a pre-civil rights black chauffeur, a regional theater understudy, a football jock and even an '80s mom. People see Beckett as the person into whom he leaps, allowing Bakula (which rhymes with Dracula) to temporarily become anyone. "I never have to be Tootsie," Bakula explains. "It's just me in the body of the mother, trying to deal with her kids, her life and whatever happens to her.

"In one episode, I play an FBI agent in the witness protection program. I leap in and am supposed to protect a woman from bad elements who are after her. It becomes a love story. I play an Indian in another episode. My grandfather is in a jailhouse and I break him out so he can go and die with his forefathers in the wilderness."

Quantum Leap benefits greatly from the levity that the ever-wry Stockwell instills in Al. It's evident that Bakula and Stockwell share a unique chemistry. "We really do have a good time. We are fortunate to have that,"

Key to the series' appeal is the rapport between Bakula and co-star Dean Stockwell (as the holographic Al).

he acknowledges. "You never know in any given situation who you're going to be cast with."

When *Magnum, P.I.* creator Don Bellisario developed *Quantum Leap*, he set certain guidelines. Beckett can only travel as far back as 1953, the year of his birth, and travel only as far forward as today. "You don't know if things have been changed in time before if they're the way they are today," explains Bakula. "Somebody could have leaped into my body yesterday and made me take a right turn. If I had made a left, perhaps I would have been killed in a car accident. But I don't know that for a fact, so as far as I know, my life is the same.

"We've gotten letters from people saying, 'How dare you break the rules of time travel!' Who *really* knows what time travel is, anyway?"

Thanks to the many other science-fiction heroes who've tripped in and out of time before, Bakula has many footprints to follow. For instance, during *Quantum Leap*'s third season, James Darren, a veteran of *The Time Tunnel*, showed up. "Darren came on the set," Bakula relates, "and we were just standing around joking about things. I said, 'So, you traveled in time?' and he said, 'Yes, I did.' I asked something like, 'Well, how was it for you?' It was a hoot!

"I'm a fan of fantasy; things like *Time Tunnel* and *Star Trek* are great. But fantasy isn't that important to me, because being an actor is already like living a fantasy; it's all flash, glitz and let's pretend. Being in *Quantum Leap*, however, gives that sense

"For an actor, Quantum Leap was a dream experience," Bakula says.

When it's mentioned to Bakula that he never really appears to be acting as Sam Beckett, he laughs, noting the compliment. "There *is* a lot of me in Sam. I like Sam's values and I like his relationships with people around him. I'm a real people person. One of the reasons I got into this business was that I really like working with people. The whole series is me getting into other people's lives and relating with the people in that person's life. I like that a lot."

Bakula frequently displayed his easy-going persona in two previous short-lived TV series, *Gung Ho* and *Eisenhower & Lutz*. Genre fans might remember his two TV movie/pilots *I-Man* ("That one had me playing an indestructible man") and *Infiltrator* (his atoms mixed with a space probe, "I became part machine and part human"). His latest genre film is writer/director Clive Barker's *Lord of Illusions*, in which he investigates a supernatural case as detective Harry D'Amour.

D'Amour seems like a man of another time. "Harry's a throwback to those classic '40s Humphrey Bogart movies," Bakula explains, "but with none of the trappings like a slouch hat or a trenchcoat. He's a good private eye with a peculiar penchant for the supernatural. It's like he's constantly drawn to the dark stuff.

"In many ways, Harry is like Sam on *Quantum Leap*. He's out there on the edge of trouble, standing between us and it. Both characters have a certain sense of reluctance about what they do."

What makes producers consider Bakula a suitable genre lead? Why is he a science-fiction hero?

"Why me? All of the roles have had some kind of quirky sense of humor attached to them. For some reason, I seem to fit that bill. It *is* actually odd if you think abut it," admits Bakula. "I love doing these roles. I have to be honest. I have a lot of the little kid in me. I love to believe these things, the science-fiction aspects, can be possible some day."

The numerous genre experiences earn Bakula the FX merit badge. "I've done a lot of them, " he understates. "*Infiltrator* was going to be television's *RoboCop*. That was done by the guys who did the robotics in *Terminator*. It was great working with them. We had wonderful people in *Quantum Leap*. Most of the FX concern Dean. The biggest special effect in this series is that I'm working with a guy who is always invisible.

"Actually, the biggest effect I'm involved with in every show are the mirror shots [in which Beckett sees the reflection of the person he's inhabiting]. They can be incredibly complicated. But when they're done right, they can be spooky and eerie and great fun."

of fantasy a real boost, because on that show I'm *always* out there in make-believe land."

Assessing *Quantum Leap*, Bakula says simply, "The show has taken many chances and managed to deliver the goods. We've never been the typical one-hour dramatic show. We've taken a very complex idea, time travel, added some innovative new elements to it and, when all is said and done, managed to get some important messages across to people while entertaining them. That's a lot to ask of any show, and I think that we succeeded more often than not."

After so many *Leaps*, Bakula does have his favorites. "I love the *La Mancha* episode because I got to sing in it. *Man of La Mancha* is one of my favorite musicals," says Bakula, who received a 1988 Tony Award nomination for his performance in the Broadway musical *Romance, Romance*. "I worked with John Cullum in that episode. I've always been a *huge* fan of his. So, that was great. I loved the episode where I played a black man. It had a lot to say and was well-handled. I like the first episode where I played a woman. That was special for television."

On *Quantum Leap,* "I'm always out there in make-believe land," Bakula notes. In this case, he's a glitter rock star.

script, saying, 'Oh, I know how this is going to end.' I never know how it's going to end."

Sam Beckett isn't the only one learning from all this leaping around. Essaying the wide variety of roles has also broadened the actor's world view. "Doing *Quantum Leap* has allowed me to get into many people's heads and play out many different situations. I know what it's like to play a black man in certain situations. I've experienced, to a degree, what the mentally handicapped go through. I've gotten a clearer picture of what it's like to be a woman. You can't help but have your opinions altered. Creating a different historical environment each week and having yourself deposited right in the middle of it has been fascinating.

"And it's not just me. Dean and I are like two kids unwrapping a present every time we get a new script. We're given new challenges every week."

Part of that challenge rests in producer/creator Don Bellisario's insistence on *not* adhering to formula.

Time ran out for *Quantum Leap*—cancelled after its fourth season. Although individual episodes have been issued on videotape and there's the vague possibility of a *Quantum Leap* movie some time in the future, the show itself ended with the ominous note that Dr. Sam Beckett never returned home.

"I'm not so sure that Sam is *ever* supposed to go back," Bakula says. "According to the way Don has set it up, Sam may be being used as an instrument of healing or humanity or justice, or whatever you want to call it. Sam's a Lone Ranger type of guy who gets in there, works out problems, and gets out. One intention seems to be that by Sam learning, he will then get back to the present. Sam learns every week, and hopefully, the viewer learns through Sam.

"One of the things that attracted me from the beginning is that Don thinks of great stories and he always puts a twist in them. So, very seldom am I sitting there while reading a

"Don isn't forcing anybody to take this show any particular way," Bakula explains. "You can watch *Quantum Leap* and be turned on by the idea of time travel and history. You can be entertained or not think of anything beyond how they got that guy to walk through a wall.

"We're like a butterfly. One week we're this, the next week we're something else. We're funny, we're serious, we're musical. Our show is a surprise every week, and we've attracted an audience that's not willing to know what's going to happen next."

In fact, Scott Bakula believes *Quantum Leap* might provide its most valuable service in stimulating fans' interest in knowing more about what already happened.

"It has been that way with me," he says. "I've become a real student of history. I'm hoping that *Quantum Leap* inspires people to turn off the television, pick up a book and talk about history. Because there's a great deal of it to talk about."

89

TIMECOP

By Kim Howard Johnson

Jean-Claude Van Damme is getting used to being a science-fiction hero. First, he was a *Cyborg*. Then, he marched as the *Universal Soldier*. And most recently, he trekked through the years as *TimeCop* and fought evil as the video game-derived *Street Fighter*.

In *Universal Soldier*, Van Damme plays Luc Devreux, a soldier in a secret government program brought back to life after more than 20 years. Van Damme and Dolph Lundgren killed each other in Vietnam, and when their memories begin returning, Van Damme escapes, accompanied by a female reporter (Ally Walker). Lundgren leads the remaining four Universal Soldiers on a chase across the southwest United States to recapture the deserter.

The film opens with Luc having flashbacks of Vietnam, and his memories are suddenly jolted. "The flashback comes to my mind. I know I died before, and I'm not the guy I'm supposed to be. I'm just escaping the battalion. A reporter has seen the action, become part of it and escapes with me. She is normal; I'm abnormal—I'm half-human and half-controlled by serum. Sometimes, she must protect me, sometimes I have to protect her. I just want to go home to see my parents. I want to pull the plug. I don't want to be part of the program.

"*Universal Soldier* is full of comedy and action and there's a long chase," says the Belgian-born star in his sometimes-thick accent. "It's like Frankenstein Jr. wants to go back home. You feel more and more sorry for the guy all through the movie. He's not the Terminator—he's a very sensitive man."

Van Damme says the diner scene is probably his favorite. As a genetically enhanced, reanimated person, he's kept alive with a special serum that keeps his body cold to prevent decomposition, but when he escapes with the reporter, his access to the serum is cut off.

"It's the first time in 25 years that I have the feeling of food in my mouth, and because I'm missing the serum, I go crazy about the food. I start to eat, and eat and eat. All these old people and rednecks are looking at me eating like a machine. The girl has left me to make some phone calls, and when she comes back, it's a mess! I kick ass, all those guys are on the floor, on the jukebox. It's crazy. I kick one guy, I eat my hot dog, then bam!" He demonstrates with a casual backhanded punch. "And I eat again. It's a great, unusual scene!"

Even though he has more of a chance to perform in *Universal Solder*, the action star never expected any awards for his work.

"It's *not* a movie that will have people saying, 'Van Damme is a fantastic actor,' because it's not enough of a part to show my emotional range. When you have an action stamp on a movie, they don't like to give awards. For example, James Cameron did *The Abyss* and *ALIENS*—to me, he's a fantastic director, but the guy has *never* won an Academy Award. They don't give Academy Awards to action films.

"*Universal Soldier* is an action film. I believe it's difficult sometimes because when you fight, you don't hit for real—you're faking the pain, the sweat, the tension. It's acting for me, but to them, it's different—it's just an action film."

Van Damme's film career has primarily involved martial arts and action, but he doesn't worry about his action image.

"I'm *not* afraid to be typecast. That doesn't frighten me. I'm very young, and I go with the script. I know right now people want me to do action films, so why should I disappoint my fans? What I would like to do is action films, plus bring in more emotions and comedy, and slowly bring in more audiences while keeping the action audience."

Van Damme and Lundgren share scenes together only in *Universal Soldier*'s beginning and end, as most of the story involves Lundgren and his soldiers chasing Van Damme. Of course, just as moviegoers expect, there's a major showdown between the pair. "The audiences want to see the fight. They want to see the challenge between Dolph and Van Damme—

Accustomed to life as a science-fiction hero, Jean-Claude Van Damme hurtles between past and future as Timecop.

Universal Soldier *Van Damme teams with reporter Ally Walker for romance on the run. "Women love the film," he asserts.*

who is going to do this, who is going to do that? It's a good attraction to the movie."

Van Damme is candid in his assessment of the film. "I liked *Universal Soldier*, but I wish we could have had more time and money for that final fight," he admits. "It was simple, like a karate contest. But, there were money problems. I wish Roland Emmerich, who's a great director [recently responsible for *StarGate*], had more time and money to do the final fight better. He was under pressure and the guy was great."

The actor believes that his character's vulnerability helped make *Universal Soldier* a success. "It was my biggest box office film ever, and in that movie, Van Damme was *not* kicking ass—he was running away!" the actor says, referring to himself yet again in the third person. "He doesn't want to fight, he's running away, he's hiding like a baby, and he doesn't know who he is—the woman's strength is what protects him. Women love the film, because they want to protect the guy. I look very vulnerable."

A native of Brussels, Van Damme moved to Hollywood in the mid-80s, and after a slow start, began finding work in martial arts and action films. He was the original *Predator*, but was replaced when lensing of the creature's scenes were delayed and the costume was changed (Kevin Peter Hall succeeded him). His first big American movie, *Bloodsport*, was followed by *Lionheart*, *Kickboxer* and the SF adventure, *Cyborg*. Van Damme co-wrote, produced and starred in *Double Impact*. His other films include John Woo's *Hard Target*, *Street Fighter* and *The Quest*.

The actor says he was relatively satisfied with his previous SF film, *Cyborg*, given the monetary restrictions.

"It cost $1.8 million. It's an OK movie for the price. You have to go at least $15 or $20 million to have something decent," he says.

In his third major genre film, *TimeCop*, Van Damme stars as futuristic policeman Max Walker, who travels from the future to prevent a corrupt politician from changing history. Along the way, Walker encounters the wife he lost years ago and must decide whether to try to change the past himself.

"I read the script in 1992, and I felt good about the film's concepts, about me traveling in the past," says Van Damme. "Of course, there was the love story as well as the action. It's a very intelligent movie, and that was a big change for my career."

Van Damme says his character copes with his wife's death by seeking refuge in his job. "Max Walker is a cop whose beloved wife died years ago," he explains. "Since she died, he was never the same, and he became a man whose only priority was his job. That's why he became such a good cop. But, he's also a guy who'll never enjoy his life anymore. He's very efficient, like a machine. Every day when he comes back home, he wants to have his past life when he was a married man, to go back and find those days. But, it's impossible."

The intricacies of time travel are dealt with in *TimeCop*, which co-stars Ron (*Lifepod*) Silver as a political candidate who travels to the past to ensure that he'll be elected in the future.

"In the film, we see that when you return to the past and try to change it, it's a very bad thing for the future," Van Damme explains. "For example, if I go back in the past, to a war where I know the strategy and troop movements, I can change those moves and win the war. That's why they have timecops, to go back to stop people who have private time machines.

"And the timecops have to do it without changing the future themselves," he adds. "When they go back to the past, they must be careful about not doing too much damage because even if they want to stop somebody who's doing something bad, they have to be careful to bring them back to the future alive with some proof so they'll be judged."

TimeCop, which also stars Mia Sara, sees Van Damme playing a character with a much softer, sentimental side.

91

His Universal Soldier alter-ego *is a very sensitive guy. "It's like Frankenstein Jr. wants to go back home," Van Damme says.*

"When I go back to my wife [Sara] in the past, there's a scene where she wants to talk to me badly. The phone rings after we're making love, and I have to go on a mission. She wants me to stay because she has to tell me something and I say, 'It can wait, I'll be back very soon.'

"She was pregnant and hadn't told me about it, so when I go back to the past, by coincidence I go back to the same day she dies. I see my younger self and her doing a test in the hospital, knowing that she's pregnant. It's such a nice scene, me knowing why she wanted me to stay at home that night, *why* she wanted it to be so romantic. It's a very touching story. We have the action for the guys, the love story for the ladies."

Van Damme believes *TimeCop* is far different from his other films. "Peter Hyams is the perfect director for *TimeCop*. He has done movies like *Outland* and *2010*. He's very good—you have to see the FX on the time-traveling sequences!"

The star says Hyams also gave him some excellent career advice. "Peter told me, 'You should spend less time training in the gym, and more time training your mouth,' learning the English and studying acting," Van Damme says. "He believes I have a shot at being not just an action star, but a French Steve McQueen!"

Van Damme is quick to point out that not only is *TimeCop* an accessible mainstream SF movie, there are some spectacular stunts. "They're great—the biggest stunts ever!" he promises. "We had one guy with his feet attached to a cable, head down. The guy was dropped for 30 floors! The cable was stopped—it was controlled by hand—about six or seven feet before touching the ground!

"Actually, that stunt involved two guys. It's a scene in the movie, where one of my old partners traveled to the past, and took a copy of *USA Today*. He came from 2008 to 1929 to buy stock that's worthless at that time, but will be worth big money in the future. He has his *USA Today*, in color, along with his Walkman. As I appear time-traveling from the future, the screen gets distorted. I say, 'I've got to take you back, man,' and he says, "No, stay away,' and he backs toward the window. He prefers to kill himself rather than come back with me. When he jumps from the window, I chase after him, catch him in the air, and we go down together But before touching the ground, we disappear into 2008! It's a great scene."

Meanwhile, Van Damme's future may eventually include a *Timecop* sequel. "I guarantee that some people will see *TimeCop* because it's a science-fiction movie, and they'll say, 'Who's that guy Jean-Claude Van Damme? That's the karate guy? I didn't know he did these types of movies!' *That* will help me to break out of action movies."

92

INDEX